"If you are feeling worn ou[t] ... be a comfort for your soul. ... Jesus anew, who sees us a[s] ... [who knows us fully, and use encoun]... grace in deeper crevices of your life, and be emboldened to live and love fully for our resurrected Jesus."

—**David Robbins**, president and CEO, FamilyLife

"I appreciate the tender ways Pastor Rivera talks about Jesus meeting us in our pain, sorrows, and doubts. I look forward to reading this book with people who don't know Christ, new Christians, and mature Christians in order to have important conversations about Christ's powerful and healing presence in our lives."

—**Dennae Pierre**, codirector, City to City North America and The Crete Collective; director, The Surge Network

"*Unexpected Jesus* is a must read! My friend Eric pours his heart out in this book as he takes you through his own stories of how Jesus has shown up in his life and uses them to help you navigate your own trials. If you have ever wanted a practical resource to help navigate Scripture and see how Jesus makes himself known in the lives of people as well as your own, then you will love this book!"

—**Derrick Puckett**, lead pastor, Renewal Church of Chicago; president, The Chicago Partnership

"Writing with the heart of a pastor, made more tender by his own experience, Eric Rivera shows how the risen Lord Jesus Christ meets us in our sorrows, disappointments, doubts, and regrets. Those who speak to human pain will always have an audience, and Eric's fresh, insightful, and heartwarming accounts of the resurrection appearances of Jesus will bring help, hope, and healing to many."

—**Colin S. Smith**, senior pastor, The Orchard Evangelical Free Church; founder and Bible teacher, Open the Bible, openthebible.org

"With the kind of pastoral concern that reflects years of ministry among people *en la lucha* (in the struggle), Dr. Eric Rivera invites readers to reflect on the questions Jesus asked the first witnesses of his resurrection. Each chapter opens with a question pulled directly from the gospels and recontextualizes them to interrogate our contemporary concerns. Dr. Rivera uses personal stories from his family and congregation to give full body testimony to the truth of the biblical narrative. *Unexpected Jesus* is a smoothly written book perfect for anyone interested in a deeper, guided devotional read."

—Emanuel Padilla, president, World Outspoken

"I love that the Lord revealed to Pastor Rivera something extraordinary from his word and he takes the time to write about it. Because of this book, we see that God is still alive and working things out, even the messy things, for our good and his glory. Eric gives us truth from God's word and even shares so many things that God has revealed about himself to him and Erikah. With every chapter you will see that God is present, that he knows every detail of your life, and that the details of your story are revealing the power of his story in you. God sees even the most complex things; he walks with you through those things and allows your story to bring hope to others by allowing them to see that God was there all along. After you read this book, share it with your family and your friends. It is truly a refuge and a builder of hope and strength for each of our troubles."

—Robyn McKelvy, author, speaker, wife, and mommy

"*Unexpected Jesus* was a sweet reminder of what happens when Jesus steps into our everyday situations! When you read this book you'll get a fresh lens into the biblical encounters with Jesus that changed peoples lives forever. Eric does a masterful job at encouraging us to see that the risen Christ desires to step into our own messy stories and infuse them with hope and encouragement."

—Lymari Navarro, writer and speaker

UNEXPECTED JESUS

UNEXPECTED JESUS

ERIC RIVERA

How the Resurrected Christ Finds Us, Meets Us, Heals Us

LEXHAM PRESS

Unexpected Jesus: How the Resurrected Christ Finds Us, Meets Us, Heals Us

Lexham Press, 1313 Commercial St., Bellingham, WA 98225
LexhamPress.com

Print ISBN 9781683596547
Digital ISBN 9781683596554
Library of Congress Control Number 2022937324

Lexham Editorial: Deborah Keiser, Allisyn Ma, Katie French
Cover Design: Joshua Hunt, Brittany Schrock
Typesetting: Justin Marr, Abigail Stocker

For Erikah,
whose tenacious faith points me
to the resurrected presence and power of Jesus.
And for Keziah, Lukas, and Levi, our treasures.

Contents

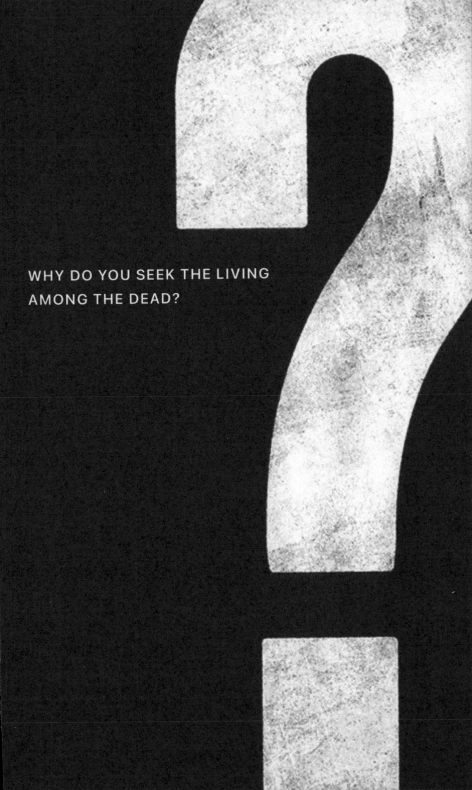

WHY DO YOU SEEK THE LIVING
AMONG THE DEAD?

1

The Resurrected Jesus Meets Us in Our Mess

Why do you seek the living among the dead?

—*Luke 24:5*

I sat in Starbucks, near our church building in Chicago, just before Easter. I was planning out my preaching calendar while reading through Jesus's resurrection appearances in the Bible. As I read, I was struck by an observation I believe the Spirit opened my eyes to see. When Jesus reveals himself to various individuals or groups of followers after raising from the dead, he includes in his conversation with them the same technique he had used throughout his earthly ministry—a question. Those questions revealed something about people's heart condition—their mess—while at the same time infusing them with the hope that only God can give.

Great teachers can capture our attention and imagination with skilled storytelling, making the complex clear and palatable. Their words have a significant effect on our lives, lingering in our heads for hours, days, and even years. If this is true of great teachers, what can be said of the greatest teacher—the Master Teacher? Jesus was the Master Teacher. His words continue to transform people's lives and have been the subject of countless studies for two thousand years.

Jesus knew how to use everyday experiences to illustrate and convey eternal truths. For example, he used a gardening metaphor to teach about the different ways people respond to the word of God (Mark 4:10–20). Jesus used a parenting metaphor to explain how our heavenly Father eagerly disseminates good gifts to his children (Luke 11:11–13). Shepherds and sheep were common sights in Israel, and Jesus compared God's pursuit of his lost follower to a shepherd searching for a lost sheep (Luke 15:1–7). Jesus even used the illustration of a traveler's mistreatment to expose racism in the human heart (Luke 10:25–37).

It's easy to imagine why many people lingered around when Jesus taught. Vast crowds enveloped him in open fields, at seashores, and along hilly terrain. His teaching was simple and creative. It was also authoritative. The Master Teacher understood the human heart in addition to knowing the will of the Father. His teaching carried a weight to it, producing conviction, comfort, challenge, and excitement. After one lengthy day of Jesus's preaching, Matthew summarizes the feeling of the crowd: "And when Jesus finished these sayings, the crowds were astonished at his teaching, for he was teaching them as one who had authority, and not as their scribes" (Matthew 7:28–29).

Common life experiences and creative metaphors were not Jesus's only tools in his toolbox. He was also an expert at asking meaningful questions. His questions silenced his critics ("The baptism of John, from where did it come? From heaven or from man?" Matthew 21:25), exposed his opponents ("Show me a denarius. Whose likeness and inscription does it have?" Luke 20:24), confronted the self-righteous ("Why do you call me good?" Luke 18:19), and lifted up the condemned ("Woman, where are they? Has no one condemned you?" John 8:10). The point of Jesus's questions was not to discover information he lacked. He knew precisely what people were thinking (John 2:24–25). Rather, his questions were a rhetorical device that revealed to the recipients what was within their hearts.

Questions have an ability to penetrate deeply into hearts in ways propositional statements or even commands do not. They beckon us to become thoughtful and introspective. When my mom asked me as a child, "Did you clean your room?" her question forced me not only to acknowledge I hadn't but to give a reason *why* I hadn't. The moment a question is posed to us we're not only given an opportunity to answer but simultaneously forced to consider why we are giving that answer.

For example, in Luke 17:11–19 Jesus enters a village and is immediately approached by ten men with a contagious skin disease. Their leprosy ostracized them from society and labeled them as "unclean." They begged Jesus to show them mercy and heal them. Jesus instructs the sick men to go to the priests, the only ones who could deem them "clean" again. They did as Jesus told them, and they were healed on the way. All ten of these men were handed a fresh start to life. It changed the rest of their lives. But the narrative gives us an interesting and unexpected detail. The passage says only one of those ten men returned to Jesus to thank him and give God praise. Jesus responds to this with a series of three questions: "Were not ten cleansed? Where are the nine? Was no one found to return and give praise to God except this foreigner?" (Luke 17:17–18). At face value, the answer to Jesus's questions were: "Yes, there were ten. I don't know where the other nine are. No one else returned to give God praise." But of course, Jesus didn't want to know where the other nine were physically at the moment. He wanted everyone who was around to understand what was taking place. At a deeper level, beyond the simple answer to the questions, was a lesson learned. The men failed to value God's healing and out of their ingratitude withheld praise to God.

Jesus Sees You

Honestly assessing our heart conditions can be a scary exercise. Like with the nine ungrateful lepers, Jesus's questions for us often reveal the miserable condition of our lives. While much of our experience is unpredictable and sometimes unexplainable, some things are constant. The human heart consistently needs God's help. Our hearts have been affected by sin and sadness, doubt and disappointment, ruin and regret, and anxiety and anger. We are often left wondering, "Can I experience joy, forgiveness, and peace?"

The fact that our hearts are a mess and our lives are messy is overwhelming. However, the same Master Teacher Jesus who asked questions to penetrate hearts is also the resurrected savior Jesus who meets us in our mess.

This was precisely the experience of Jesus's followers after his resurrection. Many of them were in dire straits as they were left reeling from the catastrophe they witnessed on Golgotha when Jesus was crucified. There they saw the one they had followed and believed in be crucified as a criminal. Their lives would have been over had the story ended there. But it didn't.

These same disciples see Jesus alive from the dead. When Jesus sees Mary Magdalene weeping by the empty tomb, he enters into her grief, asking, "Woman, why are you weeping? Whom are you seeking?" (John 20:15). Later, he finds Thomas entrenched in doubt and asks him, "Have you believed because you have seen me?" (John 20:29). Jesus meets two confused men on the road to Emmaus and inquires, "What is this conversation that you are holding with each other as you walk?" (Luke 24:16). Seven of the disciples return to fishing after the passion week events, and Jesus gets their attention with this question: "Children, do you have any fish?" (John 21:5). Consider his conversation with Peter who was neck-deep in regret: "Simon, son of John, do you love me more than these?" (John 21:15). Even Saul, who in his murderous rage seeks to arrest and harm Christians, is confronted by the resurrected Jesus. While on the road to Damascus, he sees a great light accompanied by these words, "Saul, Saul, why are you persecuting me?" (Acts 9:4).

Jesus continues to meet us in these places of grief, doubt, confusion, wandering, regret, and anger. The same kinds of questions he asked two thousand years ago are the questions he relays to us in our mess today: Why are you weeping? Do you love me? What are you doing? Why don't you believe in me? Will you trust me? Jesus's questions expose our underlying struggles and turn our eyes to him.

As a pastor, I get the privilege of leading a church family and learning their stories. It's an honor to rejoice when they celebrate and cry when they're broken. The greatest point of comfort for me, and those I minister to, is that God loves us and is near to the brokenhearted. God is present in your pain. Jesus meets you in your mess.

> God loves us and is near to the brokenhearted. God is present in your pain. Jesus meets you in your mess. Our struggles look different, and God ignores none of them.

Our struggles look different, and God ignores none of them. He invites his children to rest in him. He invites you to do that as you read this book. Perhaps you battle chronic pain and each day is a fight as you wonder why God hasn't answered your prayers. Maybe you look at life and are overwhelmingly displeased with where you're at. Perhaps you have been hurt by someone you love or find yourself in a perpetual battle with a particular sin. Or maybe you're simply not hungering for God. You're disappointed by your lack of longing and can faintly remember a time when you were passionate in your faith. Maybe you're reading this and are about ready to throw in the towel. These scenarios are messy. They're aggravating. And you may feel like you're all alone. But Jesus sees you.

In the chapters that follow, I pray you would see how the risen Jesus not only encountered his disciples in their mess but how he encounters us today. I pray God would nourish your soul and fortify your faith as you recognize you're not alone. The resurrected Jesus meets you in your mess, and because he lives, your sorrows can turn into joyful hope, your confusion into a settled trust, your doubts into secure confidence, your regret into real forgiveness, and your anger into purposeful peace.

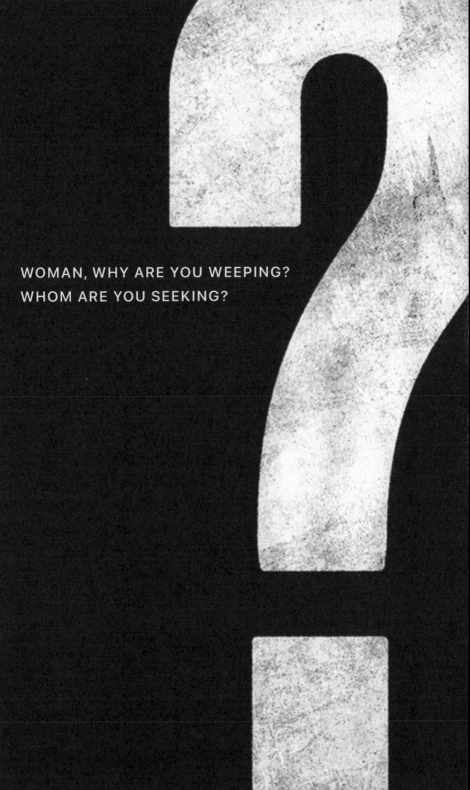

WOMAN, WHY ARE YOU WEEPING?
WHOM ARE YOU SEEKING?

2

When We Are Weeping: Jesus Comforts Us

Jesus said to her, "Woman, why are you weeping? Whom are you seeking?"

—*John 20:15*

L ate at night, I found myself on the kitchen floor, broken and weeping. I hardly had words to pray as I wrestled with fear and faith. I was overwhelmed with uncertainty. My wife Erikah was asleep in bed, and I had just tucked in our kids, fighting back tears with each prayer I prayed with them.

For over a month, life had been a series of hospital visits and tests as doctors and neurologists worked to figure out what was causing Erikah to have episodes of pain and intense fatigue. What was causing these attacks that zapped her strength for hours or days at a time?

On November 10, 2017, just a few days before Erikah's birthday, she had spinal and neurological MRIs performed. The doctor told us she would call as soon as the results were in. We left the hospital concerned but trying to stay positive. The kids and I had a great idea to throw Erikah a surprise birthday party with a few of her friends that evening. We knew this would be refreshing to her after a stressful afternoon of testing. The kids planned to dress up like waiters at a high-end restaurant and serve their mami and friends that evening. She'd love it!

We had made the twenty-minute drive home and pulled into the garage when Erikah's phone rang. It was her doctor. She told Erikah that she needed to return to the hospital immediately and be admitted. The MRIs revealed serious concerns. She needed focused medical treatment and further testing. Canceling the birthday party was the least of our worries, but it felt like yet another disappointment. Upon returning to the hospital, she underwent further testing that confirmed the diagnosis: multiple sclerosis (MS).

We had feared this outcome and prayed against it. But that day we received the diagnosis we had put in the "worst-case scenario" category when symptoms first surfaced. At the time, we wondered if life would ever be normal again. Neither my wife nor I knew how to process the news or the new reality. We were gripped by fear while trying our best to trust God.

We held tightly to the rope of God's goodness, but there were times it felt like the rope had been lathered with lotion. This is the tension that confronts us when what we know to be true of God does not appear to align with what we see with our eyes and feel in our hearts. "God, I know you are good and in control," we prayed, "but this diagnosis doesn't make sense."

Perhaps it's not a diagnosis for you, but it could be the loss of a loved one, hitting a dead end in your career that makes you feel like a failure, being rejected by someone you care about, an unrealized dream, a straying child, or an unfulfilled yearning. We will all experience sorrow and loss and find our faith pushed to what seems to be its limits. What will we do when this happens? Where will we go? To whom will we turn when the messiness of life creates genuine anguish and mourning?

Mary and Her Seven Demons

Mary Magdalene knew life-altering sadness. She was a witness to her friend Jesus's ruthless execution. She saw where his body was laid to rest and was left reeling from what she had just seen with her eyes and felt in her heart. But I imagine that her grief was far wider in scope and more cavernous in depth than the events of that grim Friday. Yet, vaster than her grief was the surpassing nature of God's goodness. When she didn't have words to pray or know what to do, Jesus would meet her in her mess.

Magdala was a small town on the western shores of the Sea of Galilee known for its fishing industry. It was only a few miles from Capernaum, the village where Jesus often ministered. Also referred to as Magadan, it was likely the hometown of Mary, whom we often know as Mary Magdalene. It was common for the place of a person's upbringing to function like a surname, identifying someone when they were away from home. Just as Jesus was known as "Jesus of Nazareth," so also was Mary of Magdala referred to by her hometown. At some point in Jesus's ministry, he meets Mary Magdalene and finds her in a treacherous predicament.

In Luke 8:2 we find out that Mary had a significant problem. She was possessed by seven demons. Demons are angelic creatures who fell from God's good presence during Satan's ancient rebellion (2 Peter 2:4; Revelation 12:9). We see in the New Testament that some demons make people deaf, unable to speak, foam at the mouth, grind their teeth, cut themselves, hate themselves, and shriek in horror. We're not told what kind of effect Mary's demons had on her, but we can extrapolate from these other examples that she must have been a frightening sight.

To intensify things, we're told that Mary had *seven* demons. The number seven in Scripture is often associated with completion and may signify that, for Mary, she was entirely under demonic influence. There are other instances in the New Testament where people have multiple demons residing in them, and they are described as unbearable to be around (Mark 5:4–6, 9). Demon-possessed individuals are enslaved and powerless to get themselves out of this peril. They need divine intervention—a bona fide miracle.

Jesus, as the incarnate Son of God, had the authority and power to perform these liberating miracles. In Mark 1:23 when a demon-possessed man comes to Jesus in the synagogue, Jesus says, "Be silent, and come out of him!" In Mark 5:8 he tells the demons that possessed a man, "Come out of the man, you unclean spirit!" Likewise, to the demon that possessed a father's child in Mark 9:25, Jesus says, "You mute and deaf spirit, I command you, come out of him and never enter him again." In these instances, and others, we see a common thread. Jesus casted out demons by the power of his word. Jesus's voice carried authority because he himself is the eternal God in human flesh.

> Jesus's voice carried authority because he himself is the eternal God in human flesh.

While we don't know the circumstances around Jesus exorcising Mary's seven demons, we can reason that Jesus's command and voice was part of it. His voice would become a treasured sound to Mary Magdalene as she proceeded to devote the rest of her life to following Jesus. Luke 8:2 tells us that several women, including Mary Magdalene, along with the twelve disciples followed Jesus in his ministry. They were a band of disciples who knew Jesus quite well. This means that Mary sat under Jesus's unparalleled teaching. She heard him speak words of forgiveness, grace, and mercy. She heard him expose sin and confront the self-righteous. She heard him talk about the kingdom of God and eternal life. She who was once an outcast and problem became accepted and an eyewitness to God's solution.

She also heard Jesus ask questions to penetrate hearts countless times. She saw Jesus transform lives just as her life was transformed. She experienced his miracles first-hand and stood in awe of Jesus as each of his disciples did. Mary hoped in Jesus. While the disciples didn't fully understand Jesus's divine identity, they believed he was the Messiah, the Savior of the world. They gave up everything to follow him. For Mary, Jesus represented hope at its highest.

You Invest in What You Believe In

Furthermore, Luke 8:3 says that women like Mary provided for Jesus and the twelve disciples "out of their means." Mary invested financially in Jesus's ministry. She gave of her personal income to monetarily support Jesus. Mary was all in!

In the 1980s there was a commercial for a product called Hair Club for Men. The chief spokesman and president of the company was Sy Sperling. Sperling would come on the commercial and list all the grand promises of the hair-growth product. He would provide scientific evidence and explain how it worked. But perhaps the greatest pitch he made in the commercial was the concluding statement. He would say, with a full head of hair, "I'm not only the Hair Club president but I'm also a client," while holding a picture of himself when he was balding. This before-and-after sight of Sy Sperling was compelling. He was able to confidently invest in and sell a product that he himself had experienced. When you know something is good, you put the energy forth to make it known.

The same could be said of Mary Magdalene. She was not only a freedom investor, but she was also a client. She not only financially supported Jesus's ministry and liberating work, she had also experienced it. She could travel with Jesus and hold up the picture of the before as she was clearly present in the after. She knew that following Jesus was a good thing.

Jesus says that the one who is forgiven little, loves little (Luke 7:47). Mary had been forgiven much and loved much. Jesus capitalizes on a real-life situation when uttering that profound truth in Luke 7:47. Jesus was having dinner at the house of a Jewish religious leader named Simon who was part of a group, the Pharisees, who had the notorious reputation of being self-righteous and lacking grace toward broken people. On this occasion at Simon's house, a "sinful" woman enters and anoints Jesus's feet with costly perfume. The word sinful implies a person of ill-repute. She may have been known for promiscuity and life of reproach. Overcome by emotion at Jesus's presence, the woman weeps and floods Jesus's feet like a steady stream. She knew her unworthiness before Jesus and could not help but bow before him. At this sight the Pharisees are livid and condemn the woman while questioning Jesus.

Jesus compares the woman to a person who is monumentally indebted to a moneylender but has their debt entirely forgiven. He contrasts that with a person who has a minimal debt to that same moneylender erased. Jesus asks Simon and the other Pharisees, "Which of them will love the moneylender more?" The answer: the person who has been forgiven more. What Mary and this "sinful woman" have in common is that they were both forgiven much and loved much.

Mary Magdalene loved Jesus deeply. She gave from her financial means to Jesus. She gave of her devotion. She ministered to Jesus's needs. She was a devoted follower like the twelve. She heard Jesus's teaching, saw his miracles, and knew his character. She was convinced that following Jesus, believing what he said, and giving all her devotion to him was the best way for her to invest her life. After encountering Jesus, Mary from the small and insignificant town of Magdala was never the same.

Like a Dreadful Text Message

Then came the crucifixion of Jesus Christ where all of Mary's hopes were dashed and immeasurable grief would greet her like a dreadful text message in the middle of the night. The Jewish authorities arrested Jesus in the garden of Gethsemane while the twelve apostles fled the scene. Peter followed from afar and John eventually arrived at Golgotha where Jesus was crucified. Ultimately, the twelve were grievously absent during Jesus's darkest hours.

It was past three o'clock on the afternoon of Good Friday when Jesus yielded up his spirit and took his last breath.

Those who were most visibly present supporting Jesus were the women. "There were also many women there, looking on from a distance," writes Matthew, "who had followed Jesus from Galilee, ministering to him, among whom were Mary Magdalene and Mary the mother of James and Joseph and the mother of the sons of Zebedee" (Matthew 27:55–56). Luke also refers to the women when he says, "And there followed him a great multitude of the people and of the women who were mourning and lamenting for him" (Luke 23:27). Mary Magdalene witnessed the horrors of Jesus's crucifixion. She saw his nail-pierced hands and feet firsthand. She saw the crown of thorns on his brow. She was there when he screamed, "My God, my God, why have you forsaken me?" (Matthew 27:46). Mary Magdalene was an eyewitness to the unfolding treachery.

Mary was up close and personal with sorrow. Jesus was the one who delivered her from the demons. He had taken her from being rejected by people to being accepted by God. She saw him take his last breath.

Mary's experience with grief is not unlike many of ours. We've been in those places where we wish we could rewind the clock and find an alternate reality—create a different world where what has transpired is not real. We can relate to Mary's empty feeling of loss and unparalleled sadness. Mary was a mess. And perhaps as you read this you confess that you also are a mess.

Let's keep this in mind. Because if we linger in the what-ifs, God's comforting hand goes unnoticed. Mary had been a mess before. And in that previous mess many years before, Jesus met her in her bondage to give her freedom. Now, in her mess of sorrow, he was about to do the same. Mary is about to encounter the resurrected Jesus who meets us in our mess. What he did for Mary, he still does for us.

It's a common misconception that followers of Jesus have their lives all together. It's a myth that pervades popular thinking, causing people to think that they need to work hard to get their life together before putting their faith in Jesus. They do this because they assume that true Christians have it all figured out. In other cases, some Christians feel discouraged because they look at people around them, who appear to be happy and unblemished, and then they look at themselves and see something different. They think if only they were good Christians like those other folks, they wouldn't be struggling with the things they fight daily. But the truth is all of our lives are messy.

Our messes may look different, but nobody has life figured out. Yes, through faith in Jesus and repentance from sin we are forgiven, made into a new creation, and have the sure confidence of eternal life. But on the flip side, we all remain works in progress. The Bible calls this sanctification.

Sanctification is the biblical teaching that acknowledges that every Christian is positionally holy before God (i.e., sanctified) based on Jesus's righteousness while also acknowledging that every Christian is to progress in holiness with the Holy Spirit's help. What this means is, until we all reach glory, we will be a sanctified mess. Or as the Protestant Reformer Martin Luther used to say in Latin, *Simul justus et peccator*, which means that we are "simultaneously righteous and a sinner." If I were preaching, I would put it this way: at the same time, we're clothed in Christ's righteousness in God's sight and a jacked-up hot mess in reality. Our messes can be a result of sin or sorrow, despair or doubt, or simply the consequence of living in a broken world as we set our eyes toward heaven. But this much is true, we are all a mess.

> Our messes can be a result of sin or sorrow, despair or doubt, or simply the consequence of living in a broken world as we set our eyes toward heaven. But this much is true, we are all a mess.

Our Backs to Jesus

On that first Good Friday, Mary Magdalene saw where Joseph of Arimathea laid Jesus's lifeless body (Luke 23:55). It happened just before sunset, which marked the beginning of the Sabbath. She returned to that same place before dawn on Sunday morning. Piecing together the exact order of events of Jesus's resurrection appearances that Sunday morning, as told in the four Gospels (Matthew, Mark, Luke, and John), has its challenges. The Gospel writers and ancient writing styles don't always provide for us the step-by-step details we want to know. For them, those aspects of the story are less important than the grander narrative, even if we wish otherwise.

The consensus is that Mary Magdalene arrived at the tomb early Sunday morning with a few other women. They saw two angels who said Jesus had risen from the grave and told them to go and tell the disciples. They were at first not struck with joyful exuberance but rather with confusion and disbelief. They left and told the disciples what they had heard. Peter and John ran to the tomb and saw it empty. Mary Magdalene returned to the tomb with Peter and John. After the two men left, Mary stood weeping outside the tomb and peeked inside.[1]

When she looked inside of the tomb Mary saw two angels who asked her why she was crying. She was overwhelmed by all that was happening and shared her sorrow over not knowing where Jesus's body was: "They have taken away my Lord, and I do not know where they have laid him" (John 20:13). Remember, Mary and the other women originally arrived at the tomb with the express purpose of anointing his dead body with spices as was the Jewish entombment custom. They did not arrive at the tomb with a resurrection anticipation but a burial responsibility. That's why Mary is still in search of Jesus's lifeless body.

We are a lot like Mary. At that moment, Mary was so set on the task of burial that she disregarded the possibility of resurrection. She wanted to know from the angels where they had placed "my Lord." Even though Jesus on several occasions talked about his impending betrayal, crucifixion, and resurrection, when the time came, his followers were not set on Jesus's promises but on the tasks and disarray before them.

We also can disregard God's words when we are distracted by tasks. Like Mary, we are guilty of ignoring God's voice. There are moments we're too busy going about our routine and handling our responsibilities to see what God is doing all around us.

Chicagoans who are accustomed to walking the city streets know they must remain keenly aware of their surroundings. In most neighborhoods, it's a matter of safety and wisdom to not let your guard down by being distracted on your phone or being so focused on where you're going that you fail to look around. As the age-old saying says, don't miss the forest for the trees. Don't get so fixated on one thing that you overlook the bigger thing. At the tomb, Mary was focused on the body of Jesus while the forest was the fact that the body wasn't missing or misplaced. It was risen!

Why Are You Weeping?

Whether Mary Magdalene had twenty-twenty vision or not, her eyes were now blurred with tears. She saw through a kaleidoscope of grief with the images around her shifting with each turn of her head. Behind her stood Jesus who asked her the same question the angels had asked, "Woman, why are you weeping?" and he added, "Whom are you seeking?" (John 20:15).

Jesus, the Master Teacher, does what he did countless times during his ministry. He penetrates the human heart with a question: "Woman, why are you weeping?" Not yet saying her name but addressing her like a stranger, Jesus's inquiry allowed her a moment to peek into her own soul. He wants Mary to understand her grief. She wept because death dashed her hopes. The one whom she loved was gone.

He follows up his first question with a second, "Whom are you seeking?" She sought Jesus, of course. However, while true that she sought Jesus, it may be asked, what *kind* of Jesus was she seeking? A lifeless Jesus or a death-conquering Jesus? A cold Jesus or a warm Jesus? By her response to the angels in the previous verses, she was looking for a breathless body. "They have taken away my Lord, and I do not know where they have laid him" (John 20:13). Jesus's series of questions reveal that Mary does not yet believe that Jesus was alive and that her profound grief resulted from the absence of lasting hope.

The details the Gospel writer gives at the tomb reveal a remarkable truth. When Mary had her eyes on her grief, she had her back to her hope—Jesus. As long as Mary kept staring into a despondent tomb, she would keep her back to her Savior. Until she turned around to look at Jesus, in the midst of her seismic sorrow, she would never experience Jesus's resurrection hope.

> Until she turned around to look at Jesus, in the midst of her seismic sorrow, she would never experience Jesus's resurrection hope.

We can hardly blame her. After all, Mary's monumental misery parallels many of our own experiences. Her grief was unexpected and untimely. Her grief was tragic and the result of something senseless.

Her grief was close to home. Jesus was a dear friend. Her grief was the product of a biased and corrupt justice system. Her grief was helpless because the circumstances around it were entirely out of her control. Her grief was firsthand as she herself witnessed the crucifixion, mockery, and brutality. Her grief was life-altering. She would never be the same. Her grief was complicated. Jesus was not only her friend, but her Lord, and her teacher. Her grief was messy. And yes, her grief was not altogether different from the grief we all experience in life.

As you read these pages you may be feeling the weight of present or past sorrow. Maybe you've been wounded by the loss of a loved one, a debilitating diagnosis, or heartbreaking news that has you reeling. Perhaps you feel the pain of being or knowing someone who is a victim of tragedy, injustice, or bias. You resonate with the complexity of sadness and feel a level of helplessness. None of us is exempt from these kinds of pains.

When Erikah began feeling the symptoms that led to her multiple sclerosis diagnosis, it seemingly came out of nowhere. It hit me like a sudden jab in the boxing ring. I reached for a spiritual wall to lean on and learned that I could take comfort that God was in control in the midst of my mess.

On October nineteenth of the fall before Erikah got sick, I wrote in my journal, "I have the promises of the gospel, your certain protection over my soul eternally and over my life until your will is accomplished in me, and your presence holding my hand through all the new and foreign seasons of life. *Increase my faith!*" Those last three words echo in my mind to this day. I didn't entirely know what I was asking for nor the means through which God would answer that prayer, but I did desire greater intimacy with God. I wanted my walk with him to deepen. This unexpected trial would be God's kind hand to grow both me and Erikah. My wife is a mighty woman of faith. She's a redwood tree in the forest, firmly anchored in Jesus and unwavering in life's storms. This precious faith and spiritual bravery blossomed in her greatest test. For both of us, through this tribulation, God increased our faith.

> He stripped us of all the things we were tempted to cling to, and we were left with Jesus. Only Jesus. Supremely Jesus! God wants us to understand that no one can encounter us and provide for us in these dark hours like he can.

Our God met us in the mess. He supplied strength when we thought we had nothing left. He allowed us to see his merciful hand at work through our loving family and church family. He stripped us of all the things we were tempted to cling to, and we were left with Jesus. Only Jesus. Supremely Jesus!

God wants us to understand that no one can encounter us and provide for us in these dark hours like he can. We need to learn what these song lyrics by Steffany Gretzinger so pointedly state,

No one ever cared for me like Jesus
His faithful hand has held me all this way
And when I'm old and grey
And all my days are numbered on the earth
Let it be known in you alone
My joy was found[2]

Isn't God so good? He places this real and personal narrative in the Scriptures to speak to us thousands of years later. As the preacher Steven J. Lawson says, "The Bible is more relevant than tomorrow's newspaper, more reliable than tomorrow's sunrise."[3] Mary Magdalene needed to know Jesus like this, just as all of us do. Had God allowed Erikah and I to keep our eyes strictly on our grief, we would've kept our backs to Jesus. Instead, God mercifully pulled us closer to himself in our scariest and most vulnerable time. What God wants us to do is understand how he meets us *in* our grief by seeing him *through* it.

Seeing Jesus with Blurred Vision

When Mary Magdalene turned around, she didn't immediately recognize Jesus. Mary supposed him to be the gardener, writes John. Perhaps Jesus veiled her eyes from recognizing him in the moment. Or perhaps her grief and expectations couldn't allow her to see a resurrected Jesus even when he stood directly in her line of sight. Her grief temporarily blinded her from seeing Jesus as our grief often inhibits our ability to see God.

But what are we to do when sorrow has blurred our vision from seeing God? How are we supposed to grasp any sort of peace when sadness keeps getting in the way? Is there an opportunity for us to have joy again? Let's look at it this way.

I have pretty bad vision. Throw in a stigmatism to that right eye and it's almost impossible for me to function without wearing my glasses or contacts and make it through a day. Without them I have to be inches from words to be able to read. I have to be within a foot of someone to make out their facial features. Sure, I can tell some people apart generally by their height or skin complexion. But if two people carry similar features and stand fifteen feet from me, it is a guessing game. However, there is one sure way for me to know who's there even with my terribly blurred vision. If I hear their voice, I know who they are.

Mary heard Jesus ask, "Why are you weeping?" and that sound didn't trigger her recognition. But when she heard Jesus say her name, "Mary," her sorrows were subdued and the clouds of sadness gusted away by the power of Jesus's voice. Mary's puffy eyes and dull ears couldn't keep out the sound of Jesus saying her name. When the sorrows of life blur your vision, trust the guidance of God's voice.

Mary knew that voice. That was the voice she heard when her seven demons were released. That was the voice she heard when she was summoned to follow Jesus. That was the voice she heard at the Sea of Galilee teaching the crowds, in the town synagogues unpacking the Torah, and in households giving hope. That is the voice our ears must be attuned to hearing, especially when life hurts.

God has spoken through his word and continues to speak. His promises jump off the pages of Scripture. His character and declarations are there in plain sight. The Holy Spirit impresses the Bible's teachings upon our hearts embracing us with its truths. There, the voice of God speaks to us in our mess. Just as Jesus knew and spoke Mary's name, he also knows and speaks your name. You are not a statistic, an object, or an unknown. Rather, you are known and personally valued by your Savior who breaks through your blurred vision and speaks to you in your grief.

> You are known and personally valued by your Savior who breaks through your blurred vision and speaks to you in your grief.

Mary explodes with unobstructed hope at this impossible realization. This was no gardener. Jesus's body had not been taken anywhere. The tomb was empty, but not because his body was removed. The tomb was empty because Jesus was alive. And he met her right there and then. When she was focused on the task of anointing his buried body, God was working all around her. While she was neck deep in a sea of grief, Jesus met her with life-preserving peace. Mary cries, "Rabboni," which means teacher in Aramaic. She knew beyond a shadow of a doubt that this was Jesus standing in her midst, in her mess.

Gladness Followed by Going

Jesus tells Mary, "Do not cling to me, for I have not yet ascended to the Father, but go to my brothers and say to them, 'I am ascending to my Father and your Father, to my God and your God" (John 20:17).[4] It's likely that Mary threw her arms around Jesus in joyful exuberance, as the disciples do in Matthew 28:9. She didn't want that moment to end. We wouldn't expect otherwise. When despairing grief turns into peace, we want to throw down our anchor and stay there as long as we can.

What Jesus addresses by saying, "Do not cling to me," is not the embrace, but the desire to linger. Although this was a celebratory moment for Mary to enjoy, there was good news for her to share with others. The resurrected Jesus would only be around for less than six weeks. His resurrection set off a timeline leading to his ascension where he finally was lifted up before their sight forty days later (Luke 24:50–53; Acts 1:9–11).

Jesus gave Mary the task of being the very first evangelist. She had resurrection news that no one else knew about. The women were the first to see the risen Jesus, and Mary was the first of the women. Even though the testimony of women was not valid in Jewish courts, God, in subversive fashion, simultaneously validates the women and announces his good news. These women were the ones he chose. God hand-picked them to be the ones to declare the resurrection, sharing the message that would change the world.

Jesus loved us so much that he died in our place for our sins and rose from the dead to offer us mercy and eternal life if we would put our faith in him and turn back to God. This is the offer of salvation God presents to us. We who were spiritually dead are now spiritually alive. The old us is gone and the new us has come (2 Corinthians 5:17). We have a relationship with God almighty and with this identity comes adoption into God's family (Romans 8:14–16). We are sons and daughters of God which makes the people of God our brothers and sisters. In both John 20:17 and Matthew 28:10, Jesus tells Mary to "go and tell my brothers" what has happened. He calls the disciples "my brothers," an identity made possible by his resurrection. We are now all family.

Seeing Hope through the Pain

Jesus wants Mary to return to the "brothers" with a message—"Go and tell." "Go" is God's command for all who have experienced his goodness in the mess of life. It's not in the DNA of a person who's encountered the resurrected Jesus to remain silent. Mary couldn't be stationary. She had to go to the disciples and tell them this good news.

I like to imagine what it was like when Mary burst through the room where the disciples were. "I have seen the Lord!" She saw him! Yes, through blurry, tear-soaked eyes. Yes, through grief-stricken sorrow. But she saw him. He met her. Jesus came to Mary Magdalene on her saddest day and her message was simple, but life-giving. She saw him. The disciples were confronted with a new reality from a trusted source, their friend Mary.

When sorrow meets Jesus, it produces a testimony. This doesn't mean that grief will instantly disappear. But it means that your blurred eyes can still see Jesus. And others with blurred eyes need to hear about how Jesus broke through your sorrow and can do the same for them. When their eyes remain focused on grief, they will have their back to Jesus. But when our puffy eyes look at Jesus, we can see hope through the pain.

If He Can Do It for Magdalena,
He Can Do It for Me

When I first met Ana she was quiet but not shy. She had an expectant smile, clearly feeling as if she was in our church building with a real purpose. Ana came to our church at the invitation of my mom and dad. They met Ana at a clinic where both she and my mom were having procedures done for chronic pain. Ana saw my dad reading a book on heaven and asked him what it was about. My dad, being the outgoing person that he is, engaged Ana in a conversation about his faith and encouraged her to visit, which wasn't far from where they were. Ana didn't visit. At least not right away. Several months went by and Ana returned to the clinic for a follow-up appointment only to run into my parents again. I'm not kidding. My mom proceeded to invite Ana to our church, and this time Ana agreed. So, there she was, the following Sunday, sitting with expectant hope.

Ana was processing life. She had gone through a lot of personal struggles. She had pain related to her sciatic nerve. She was longing to break through the chains of alcohol addiction in addition to trying to figure out her own identity. Life became overwhelming for her, and she felt as if she lived at the intersection of grief and pain. Truly, she was at a crossroad.

Not long after Ana first connected with our church family, she heard about Mary Magdalene during a Sunday sermon and the way Jesus encountered her after his resurrection—in her mess. She felt a sense of solidarity with Mary. Ana's story of searching and sorrow was not altogether different from Mary Magdalene's experience of despair and dejection.

After service, Ana lingered in our fellowship hall talking with people and enjoying interactions with our church (we're a predominantly Latino church, so we love to talk and hang out over *pan y café*—bread and coffee). As the crowd got smaller, Ana signaled for me to sit down and talk with her. She had tears in her eyes as she shared with me that she had placed her faith in Jesus, surrendering her life to Christ at the end of the service. I couldn't contain my joy. Ana reflected on Jesus's deliverance of Mary's demons, Mary's new life in Christ, and the joy of Jesus's resurrection. Ana then told me something that I'll never forget. She said, "If he can do it for Magdalena, he can do it for me." That's just it! Ana understood that Mary Magdalene's story wasn't an anomaly. Whether it's a Jewish woman like Mary in the first century or a Puerto Rican woman like Ana in the

twenty-first century, God encounters us the same. Mary's
experience of joy in her messy grief can be our experience
of joy in sorrow.

From the Scent of Death to
the Fragrance of Life

It's not rare for there to be in a church a person who's experienced profound suffering and pain, and yet who demon-
strates unparalleled faith. Sometimes it's a single parent or
widow. Sometimes it's a humble laborer or an elderly couple.
Like Mary Magdalene, they are familiar with suffering. Grief
is far more than a casual acquaintance to them—more like a
deeply personal relationship. These dear ones will tell you
how God pulled them through. They'll tell you how much
the risen Jesus means to them and how God's presence is
what sustains them. They're often the mighty prayer war-
riors in the church. They're the ones who speak Scripture
like a second language. They have a kind of peace that only
comes from seeing Jesus in the midst of their mess. They
will tell you, if it wasn't for the pain, they wouldn't know
Jesus as intimately as they do. When your eyes are on Jesus,
their experience can be yours.

Mary's life was radically changed when Jesus cast the
demons out of her. But her life would be changed for eternity when Jesus rose from the dead. Her grief in life was met
with resurrection hope. When Mary arrived at the tomb, she
expected to find the scent of death, not the fragrance of life.
She expected to find a lifeless corpse, not a life-changing

conversation. She expected to find a crucified body, not a familiar voice. Jesus exceeded her expectations and brought her a kind of comfort only God can deliver.

As you experience the trials of life, God will meet you in ways you may not expect. Although what you know to be true may not align with what you see with your eyes and feel in your heart, set your eyes on Jesus and tune your ears to his voice. Let the word of God be your guide as the Holy Spirit brings you comfort. Because he lives, your sorrow can turn into joyful hope.

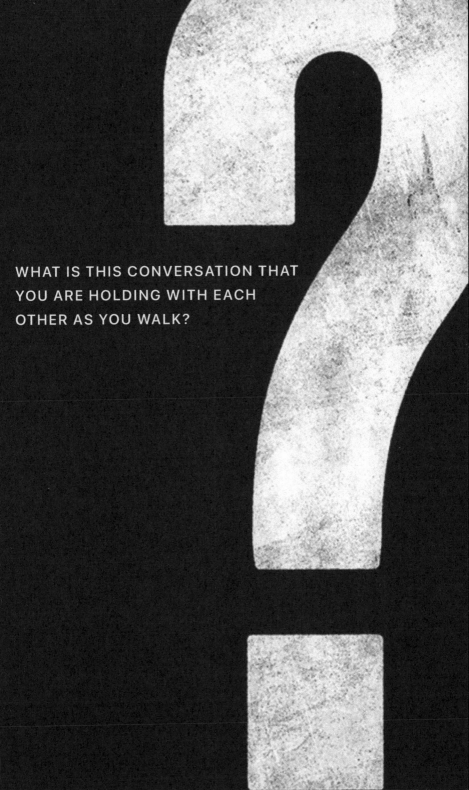

WHAT IS THIS CONVERSATION THAT
YOU ARE HOLDING WITH EACH
OTHER AS YOU WALK?

3

In Our Hopelessness: Jesus Lights Our Heart

And [Jesus] said to them, "What is this conversation that you are holding with each other as you walk?" And they stood still, looking sad.

—*Luke 24:17*

If you ever get the chance to visit Israel, jump on the opportunity. In 2019, Erikah and I were able to do just that. We won't forget savoring the aroma in the markets and the flavors of the foods like shawarma, falafel, and tabbouleh. And we can't say enough about the experience of visiting many biblical locations from the Sea of Galilee in the north to the Mount of Olives in the south, the Jordan River to the east and the Mediterranean Sea to the west. We relived dozens of Bible stories in our imaginations.

One day we visited Jerusalem and went underground into what is called Hezekiah's Tunnel. At various places in this tunnel system things got pretty tight. The tunnels became narrow and the walkway constricted. There were places where our shoulders nearly touched both walls at the same time. It was the kind of space that would make most people feel uncomfortable and even claustrophobic. The tour guide warned us about this ahead of time and gave us some pointers before entering. "Don't panic. Just keep walking," he told us. Even though we couldn't see the proverbial "light at the end of the tunnel," we knew that the tunnel system would eventually widen and take us back to the surface. All we needed to do was keep our eyes on what was ahead and continue walking.

In life, when pressures mount, it feels as if the walls are closing in on us. Few things can do that like crushed hopes. When the things we anticipate and the dreams we've envisioned come to a sudden or gradual halt, we lose heart. Sometimes these dashed hopes come in the form of relationships that don't materialize, careers that become a dead end, education that has left you underemployed, unemployed, or debt-ridden. Maybe the most desperate of all forms of hopelessness is when we feel as if God himself has failed to deliver on our expectations. Perhaps you've hoped in God and trusted him and believed he was going to answer your prayers or come through in miraculous ways, and he hasn't. When these realities don't match your anticipations, you are left with an acute disappointment—wondering what's next.

Corridors of Reflective Anguish

We had been married for just over two years when Erikah and I were ready and eager to start a family. We thought conceiving would come quickly, but that was not the case for us. We tried for months and were beginning to be concerned. We had to ward off the fears and insecurities that lurked in our minds. Finally, the following spring, we had a pregnancy test read positive. We had a doctor appointment shortly after which confirmed the pregnancy test. This was thrilling for us. Bursting with excitement, within days we told our immediate family. But that thrill didn't last long. We were only halfway through our first trimester when my wife began to bleed. Something wasn't right. We scheduled an appointment with our doctor, praying that our baby was okay. But the baby wasn't. The ultrasound technician could not pick up a heartbeat no matter how hard she tried. We had a miscarriage. In an instant, all our longings and all our hopes were crushed. We were devastated. We felt completely abandoned by God and confused. So confused. What was joyous quickly turned into a mess. A mess of sorrow, disappointment, confusion, and resentment.

What situation comes to your mind when you were painfully confused by God's sovereignty? Like us, you probably felt like the walls were closing in on you. As much as we wanted to be strong in our faith, we quickly learned how weak we were. Disappointment can cut deep, especially when our hopes were at their pinnacle. Remarkably, but not surprisingly, even still, Jesus can meet us in the midst of this confusion and potential for disillusionment. He can stand with us amid what at first glance appears to be a hopeless mess.

In Luke 24 we find two men who articulate their disappointment with God with three simple words—"we had hoped." Cleopas and his friend, whose name isn't given, left Jerusalem the Sunday after Jesus's crucifixion for a two-and-a-half-hour walk to a town called Emmaus about seven miles away. As they journeyed, they replayed the events of Good Friday, the Sabbath, and what they heard early that Sunday morning. They saw Jesus on the cross. He was truly dead when the guards took him down and laid him in Joseph of Arimathea's tomb. But to complicate their emotions, they heard that morning that his tomb was empty and that angels told their friends that Jesus was alive. Confusion gripped them as hope dissipated.

These corridors of reflective anguish are paths we long to dodge but oftentimes find unavoidable. However, the road to Emmaus doesn't end the same way it began. Although Cleopas and his friend commenced their journey in a despondent mess, their conversation would soon take a turn even if the actual road did not.

What's Going On?

In the narrative the resurrected Jesus asks these men three pertinent and strategically placed questions. "What is this conversation that you are holding with each other as you walk?" (24:17), asked the unfamiliar voice. Cleopas and his friend were suddenly accompanied by an inquisitive traveler who wanted in on their exchange. I'm not sure I would've been as patient with this nosy stranger. In fact, I find myself getting agitated by questions when I'm most discouraged by life. But they indulge this man's inquiry. The stranger heard some of what they had discussed, which is why they were surprised that he didn't know what was going on. Cleopas answers his question with a question of his own, "Are you the only visitor to Jerusalem who does not know the things that have happened there in these days?" (24:18).

In a glorious display of God's compassion, this stranger knew exactly what was going on because this traveler was the resurrected Jesus himself. In the moments when their hope drifted from them, hope incarnate walked with them. That's our God.

It's important for us to remember that even though we may not be able to see clearly, that doesn't mean God isn't at work. God may not always show up in the ways we want him to or expect him to, but that doesn't mean he stands idly by, disinterested in our concerns. Jesus's choice to meet the two men on the road to Emmaus is a remarkable turn of events. However, equally remarkable is the fact that they don't recognize Jesus *and* that Jesus is in no rush to reveal himself to them.

> God may not always show up in the ways we want him to or expect him to, but that doesn't mean he stands idly by, disinterested in our concerns.

Rather than immediately making sense of their confusion, Jesus begins a conversation when he asks about their discussion. His question invites them to articulate their distress. Jesus wants them to unveil the point of their confusion, even if sharing hurts. Just as treating an infected wound is painful, it's also necessary for proper treatment that leads to genuine healing.

In verse 16, Luke tells us that "their eyes were kept from recognizing him." The words "were kept" in the Greek are a single verb, *ekratounto,* that carries the idea of something "restrained" or "prevented." It's also written in the passive voice, which means that this action of "restraining" was done to them and not by them.[5] Essentially, something outside of them, perhaps their sorrow, their preoccupation, or their weariness prevented them from recognizing Jesus. As this story unfolds, it becomes quite clear that it is God that prevents them from recognizing Jesus in that moment.

Jesus wouldn't be out-questioned by Cleopas. He responds to Cleopas's question, which was an answer to Jesus's original question, with yet a second question. Jesus asks them, "What things?" What had happened in the previous days? They told him about Jesus from Nazareth, his powerful works and his remarkable teaching. They also explained to this traveler about Jesus's crucifixion at the hands of their religious leaders. But most heart-piercing is what we read in verse 21 when they added, "But we had hoped that he was the one to redeem Israel." They thought he was the one who would make everything right.

The Jews knew that God had promised a Messiah would come from the line of David and reign as a king, succeeding in ways not even David could. The Messiah would crush Israel's enemies and establish a kingdom where righteousness and justice prevailed. In the first century, the hope for the coming of the Messiah was viewed against the backdrop of Roman oppression. The Roman Empire was mighty and Israel was weak. The Jewish people were subjugated to Caesar's rule and oppressed by the tyranny of local officials. The children of Israel longed for the Messiah to liberate them, to redeem them, and to govern over them with gracious authority ushering in a time of shalom—genuine prosperity and peace for the nation. Cleopas and his friend sincerely believed that Jesus was the one to do this.[6]

Were they naïve? Was their hope in Jesus misplaced? Of course not. They had every reason to believe in him. They saw him live his life. He never lied, never gossiped, and was never greedy or arrogant. Jesus fed the hungry, was gentle with children, and respected and validated women in a culture that minimized them. He hated evil and was enraged by the religious leaders who abused the marginalized. Jesus taught the Scriptures with convincing persuasion. People marveled when he opened his mouth. He healed sick people. He turned water to wine. They knew he had calmed the sea in the middle of a storm. They knew that he had even raised the dead. They had every reason to hope in him. They were not naïve. Rather, they were hopeful Jews who believed in

Jesus. But now this all felt uncertain. Their faith was demoralized, leaving them baffled.

Learning to Trust God on
Your Emmaus Road

Knowing the extent of Cleopas's and his friend's dejection, why would God conceal Jesus's identity before them? Doesn't he want to restore their hope? Doesn't he want their pain to go away? Doesn't God care about the things that don't make sense to us and make us dejected? As we see with each of Jesus's resurrection appearances, he doesn't always operate in ways we might expect. He's countless steps ahead of us, working out something that we can't immediately see. It's undeniable that had they recognized Jesus, the exchange that followed their initial encounter would have gone in an entirely different direction. God was more concerned about the gradual revelation that would take place through the conversation than the revelation that could come from an instant illumination of Jesus.

Let me say it this way. God's plan was for their hopes to be restored not at the snap of a finger but through a discussion. Through their dialogue with Jesus, they will *see* in unique ways God's grand redemptive plans that they would not have *seen* had Jesus simply said, "Hey, look! It's me, Jesus!"

Could it be that God wants you and I to experience his hope in the midst of our discouragement rather than an instant deliverance from the things that weigh on us? Could it be that God isn't giving you the full picture and meeting your expectations because he wants to broaden your point of view and teach you to trust him?

When Erikah and I were first married, it was our plan for me to begin a seminary education just over a year after our wedding. Although we wanted to stay in Chicago, it seemed like the best school options would relocate us out of state. There was one school, however, in the northern suburbs of Chicago that was on the top of my preference list but at the bottom of my reality list. Trinity Evangelical Divinity School's Master of Divinity program seemed to perfectly fit the ways I needed to grow during my preparation for pastoral ministry. A bonus was that we could still live in Chicago and commute to class. However, there was one major problem. The school was out of our financial range. Although I really wanted to go there, we couldn't justify the price tag. Because of that, I didn't apply for the school and essentially brushed it aside. I didn't want that disappointment to affect me.

However, during my seminary search, I found out about a full-tuition scholarship that Trinity had and immediately began to pursue it. This was it. This was going to be the way God would move to pay for my graduate school education while allowing us to remain in Chicago. I applied for the school and for the full-ride scholarship. Several weeks later I received a letter in the mail that contained both good news and bad news. The good news was that I had been accepted into the Master of Divinity program. The bad news was that I was denied the scholarship. I don't think I can put into words how deflating that letter was for Erikah and me. We thought this would be the way God kept us in Chicago, got me into my choice school, and paid for my education. Instead, it felt like a cruel, celestial bait and switch. I was frustrated and highly discouraged.

My eyes were not able to see how God was at work. Sure, God could have given us that scholarship, but at that time of our lives, he wanted to teach us a lesson on how to trust him day by day. I was accepted into the school I wanted to be at, but I didn't have the means to actually enroll there. Erikah and I began to crunch numbers and discovered that between our savings account and our annual income we could cover the cost of my first year of seminary. But how would we pay for year two? The resounding answer we sensed God telling us was to trust him and watch him provide. Through prayer and the counsel of others we did just that, and in the process we learned a lot about walking by faith, being frugal, maintaining generosity, and trusting God one day at a time.

We were able to live in Chicago and I made the commute for the next three years, which kept us in our church community and the city to which we believed God had called us. God had a plan that featured disappointment but would be used to teach us to trust him. Our home church hired me as an associate pastor upon completing seminary, and from there, God opened doors for us to plant our current home church, The Brook, in 2013. I couldn't see these things when I

was denied the scholarship, but
God could. For Cleopas and his
friend, for Erikah and me, and
for you, God will walk alongside
you through the days of disappointment and dashed hopes
and use them to form your faith.

> God will walk with you
> through the days of
> disappointment and
> dashed hopes and use
> that to form your faith.

Slow to Believe

Rather than immediately reveal himself, Jesus engages the
men in a conversation. He listens to their baffled thoughts
before offering this rebuke, "O foolish ones, and slow of
heart to believe all that the prophets have spoken!" Jesus
calls them foolish not as a word of insult but as a show of
astonishment over their inability to connect the dots. Jesus
believes these men already had all of the information and
facts needed to discern what God was doing and believe the
testimony of the women. Notice what Jesus is rebuking. It's
not their lack of understanding as much as it is their unbelief.
They knew what the women had said concerning an angelic
messenger who told them Jesus was alive. Their struggle was
believing what they heard from the women. Jesus knew their
hearts. Their problem wasn't a lack of information, but a
belief in the information they had. The prophetic roadmap
of the Old Testament Scriptures led directly to the destination in which they found themselves at that moment.

Jesus, the Master Teacher, follows the rebuke with his
prototypical heart-penetrating question, his third question

in this narrative. He asked, "Was it not necessary that the Christ should suffer these things and enter into his glory?" (Luke 24:26). In this case, the question feels more rhetorical in nature. Rather than seeking a yes or no, he wants them to do a mental recall of Old Testament promises like someone scrolls through a text thread looking for a forgotten message. Jesus's question implies, "God said this would all take place. It's right there in the Scriptures. It's all going precisely according to God's plan." In fact, it was not only God's plan, but it was *necessary* for the plan to unfold in this way. The pump has been primed. It's time for Jesus to start the engine and make plain what they are being slow to see and slow to believe.

Hope Is Rising

Jesus began to explain to them from the writings of Moses (Genesis through Deuteronomy) onward how what they saw happen at the cross was all part of God's redemptive plan. The Bible is comprised of sixty-six books written over a 1,600-year period by over forty human authors inspired by God testifying to his story of redemption. All thirty-nine books of the Old Testament point to Jesus. All twenty-seven books of the New Testament unveil his life and work. Jesus's shadow is cast upon every page. He is the climax of Scripture. And now, the pinnacle of revelation walked with these two men. Jesus wanted Cleopas and his friend to not only know that he was alive but understand why he had to die in the first place.

It reminds me of my mother-in-law who was raised in the Catholic church regularly saying the Lord's Prayer and hearing the words, "Behold, the Lamb of God, who takes away the sins of the world," before each communion. It wasn't until a friend shared with her the good news of Jesus in such a way that spoke to her where she was at in life that she was convicted of her sin and put her full faith in Jesus. She said the next time she took communion, she was gripped by the truths she had repeated and heard all her life. The truth had always been right there before her, but it was as if it was hidden in plain sight. She needed the Holy Spirit to open her eyes and awaken her heart to these glorious truths.

Cleopas and his friend learned that Jesus had to die. It was all part of God's design to save humanity from their sin, defeat the evil one, and conquer death. To their amazement, in the moment when life didn't make sense and disappointment was at its pinnacle, they heard that God was firmly in control. Everything was going precisely according to God's plan. They didn't begin the conversation with a category in their mind for a suffering Messiah, let alone a resurrected one. So, as the story of redemption slowly unfolds, they are left bewildered.

This kind of bewilderment happens when our hearts are sickened by deferred hope (Proverbs 13:12) but something in our situation changes and the Spirit tells us, *Don't give up just yet.* These are crucial moments where we must believe God even when we can't fully see what he's doing. When we hold on to his gospel promises revealed from Genesis to Revelation and take him at his word, then and only then will we see God's hand, even if we never fully understand what has taken place in our minds and hearts.

We enjoy road trips as a family. From Chicago, we've driven to Washington D.C., to the Rocky Mountain National Park in Colorado, to the Black Hills of Tennessee, and all the way to Tampa, Florida. When you are the driver on a road trip, the last thing you want to do is stop. You want to cover as much ground as you can until someone in your vehicle needs a bathroom break. On one occasion we had just filled up the gas tank in preparation for a long stretch of driving. Hours had gone by and remarkably no one needed a pit stop so I pressed on. The family had fallen asleep, and I wanted to get as far as I could. The gas gauge slowly decreased without me paying much attention to it. That is, until the gas light went on. Suddenly, I realized I needed to get to a gas station ASAP. The problem was that we were in the middle of nowhere. I strained my eyes looking for that blue highway sign indicating a gas station at the next exit. That sign was not in sight. I became nervous thinking, what do we do if the car stops? I became frustrated with myself for getting into this situation. I prayed tenaciously and peered desperately. After several miles of this anxious eye-squinting, I saw that precious blue sign signaling to me that a gas station was only a few exits away. The sign made me hopeful, but our van still needed to get there. As an answer to prayer, we made it. I wasn't completely at ease until I pulled off at the exit and saw the gas station with my own eyes, but when I did, desperation turned into relief.

This was not all that different from Cleopas and his friend's experience. After hearing the stranger explain God's truth, the Emmaus road travelers had reason to hope, but they still needed to see Jesus with their own eyes. They needed confirmation that they could believe in the idea of a resurrected Savior. Jesus knew this and would soon let them see him, turning their desperation into relief.

Burning Hearts

The seven-mile trip reached its conclusion as they approached Emmaus. It was now Sunday evening. The stranger gave the two men the impression he would continue on the road to another destination, but they urged him to lodge with them for the night in Emmaus. Jesus obliged. This too was part of God's plan. He wasn't done with the followers.

The group sat down to share a meal, undoubtedly fatigued by the journey but perhaps also invigorated by the remarkable Bible explanation they just received. While the invitation to spend the night in Emmaus was a common display of hospitality in Jewish culture, what took place next flipped the script. The house guest became the meal host.

While saying a blessing over the meal was the responsibility of the head of the household, Jesus was the one who "took the bread and blessed and broke it and gave it to them" (Luke 24:30). In a sense, they were in Jesus's home. "The

earth is the LORD'S," says the psalmist, "and everything in
it" (Psalm 24:1 NLT). After all, Jesus is the one who created
the world (Colossians 1:16) and upholds the universe by
the power of his word (Hebrews 1:3). All things were made
through him, and nothing that has been made was done so
apart from him (John 1:3).

The verbs that Luke uses to describe Jesus's actions are
important. The action of taking the bread, blessing it, breaking it, and giving it recalls two instances where Jesus does
the same thing right before making a great revelation.[7]

In Luke 9:10–17, we read the narrative of Jesus attracting
a large crowd of about five thousand people who are now
hungry from a long day of teaching. The disciples suggest
Jesus send the crowd away to find food, but Jesus intends
to feed the crowd himself. Two fish and five loaves of bread
are gathered from the crowd. With it, Jesus will satisfy
their physical hunger as he had done their spiritual appe-
tite. Jesus, taking the loaves and fish, looked up to heaven,
said a blessing, broke the loaves, and gave the food to the
crowd. Everyone marveled. In the ensuing verses, Jesus asks
the disciples, "Who do the crowds say that I am," and "who
do you say that I am?" At that moment God gives Peter a
glorious realization about Jesus: he is "the Christ of God."
The breaking of the bread was followed by divine revelation.

Similarly, in Luke 22:14–23, Jesus is with his disciples during the Passover meal the night he was betrayed
by Judas. There, Luke says that Jesus took the bread, gave
thanks, broke it, and gave it to them. The first Lord's Supper

foreshadows Jesus's broken body and shed blood that would take place just hours later. Jesus tells them this is the "new covenant" to be accomplished by his death. Again, the breaking of the bread gives way to divine revelation.

Now, in that Emmaus home, Jesus's breaking of the bread opened their eyes to see and recognize this once-strange traveler. Divine revelation followed. For the first time, Cleopas and his friend recognize Jesus. God, at that moment, opened their eyes. It was him! All along, on the road as they walked and their hopes were dashed, Jesus was there. He was right by their side when they were utterly confused. Yes, he let them go through this trial. But it was necessary for them to "suffer" so they could fully under-stand Jesus's suffering, death, and resurrection as part of God's plan.

Upon revealing himself to them, Jesus doesn't linger. In a snap, he vanishes from their sight. For the moment, he completed the work he set out to do in illuminating God's plan before revealing his identity. Neither man complained. Rather, they marvel at what they learned. They confess, "Did not our hearts burn within us while he talked to us on the road, while he opened to us the Scriptures?" (Luke 24:32).

No wonder their "hearts burned" as Jesus unpacked God's plan to save them. It was not a plan to save them from Roman oppression, but a plan to save them from a viler foe—separation from God. Although the blazing fire of confidence in Jesus became nothing but a smoldering wick when he died, the resurrected Jesus was oxygen to the weakened flames. The embers of their belief began to burn more intensely once their eyes were opened. This belief was gas on the fire, and their faith was set ablaze. Hope was being resurrected from the graveyard of despair. They suddenly went from being "ear-witnesses" of the resurrection to eyewitnesses of it. Jesus was alive, and they saw him with their own eyes!

Like the friends of Jesus, when uncertainty leaves us in darkness, we may not see the resurrected Jesus in bodily form. But what we can do is know he is with us. As followers of Jesus today, even when confused, he will strengthen us to walk by faith and not by sight with these assurances. We have the gospel message of Jesus's life and death along with the sure hope of his resurrection. We have the inward testimony of the Holy Spirit confirming in our hearts that we belong to God and he will never leave or forsake us. We have the written word of God, the Bible, where God's promises are declared and his trustworthy character is displayed. We have a history of redeemed peoples from tribes, tongues, and nations throughout the world whose stories of faith and trusting God in the deepest disappointments enrich our faith. We have our own changed lives. The same God who loves us and took us from the pit of our mess and delivered us from our greatest foe is the

> Jesus is alive, and we can see him at work with our own eyes. He journeys with us, calling us to trust him—to take him at his word by holding on to his promises.

God who will see us through our discouragements and most heartbreaking unmet expectations. Jesus is alive, and we can see him at work with our own eyes. He journeys with us, calling us to trust him—to take him at his word by holding on to his promises.

He Left, and So Would They

Good news can't be contained. We can't bottle it up and keep it to ourselves. Each time the disciples saw the resurrected Jesus, they were moved to immediate action. Cleopas and his friend didn't linger in Emmaus. "That very hour" they got back on the road to Jerusalem to tell the disciples what happened (Luke 24:33). Even though the distance didn't change, their disposition did. Joyful journeys feel shorter than grief-stricken ones. Both, however, are part of life. Jesus is no less with us in our sorrow than in our joy.

When they found the disciples, they gathered and talked, putting together the fragments of the weekend like a thousand-piece puzzle. When you first pour out the pieces of a puzzle on a table, it appears to be an impossible mess. It isn't until you start connecting the more obvious pieces, little by little, that an image begins to form and the puzzle starts taking shape. By piecing things together, they began to see the picture clearer.

Cleopas and his friend probably rushed into the room, saying, "You're not going to believe what just happened to us," only to hear the disciples reply, "No, you are not going to believe what happened to us!" They told the two men

that Jesus had appeared to Peter—the most prominent of
the disciples. Cleopas and his friend share what happened
to them, and for everyone in the room, the puzzle begins
to look like the image on the box. It was all connecting. The
resurrection truly took place. The grave suffered a chilling
defeat.

Jesus Walks

It was May 2006 when we learned about our miscarriage.
What followed was a wilderness of confusion. We didn't give
up our faith in God, but it took a substantial hit. It's hard to
pray when you're confused. It's hard to trust when you've
been let down. It's hard to relate to others when they seem
so happy. It was hard for me to relate to Erikah. Her grief
was different than mine. It had a different kind of depth
and constancy. I didn't know how to be there for her. But
God did. Jesus walked with her on her Emmaus road as he
walked with me on mine. Like our experience in Israel, even
though we felt claustrophobic from this trial, we needed to
keep walking with our eyes set on Jesus.

Jesus walked with us in his word. We read the book of
Job in the ensuing months and were comforted that God was
in control, even when our world was spinning. Jesus walked
with us through worship. These song lyrics by Jeremy Camp
were almost on repeat either literally in our living room or
in my mind: "I will walk by faith, even when I cannot see,
because this broken road, prepares your will for me."[8] God
had never let go of us. Jesus walked with us through the

godly people that surrounded us, speaking life and hope to our disappointed hearts. Jesus walked with us through the comforting presence of the Holy Spirit, reminding us of his promises and graciously giving us peace that surpasses all understanding (Philippians 4:7). In the same way, Jesus will walk with you through his word, prayer and worship, a biblical church community, and the Holy Spirit's peace-giving work.

As we journey down the Emmaus road, God wants us to know that he's in control. He holds history in his hands and orchestrates events according to his good and gracious will. It's true that sometimes you will be left wondering why things happen. Life gets messy and the mess produces confusion and disappointment. Let Cleopas and his friend's experience remind you that the resurrected Jesus will meet you in your mess. He wants to create a category in your heart and mind that allows you to rest in the fact that God is in control even when things don't make sense. God wants to open your ears and eyes to the resurrected Jesus. He wants his promises to burn in your heart, especially when life is most perplexing and overwhelming. When life causes you to feel dejected, he wants hope to rise. Because Jesus lives, your confusion can turn into steadfast trust.

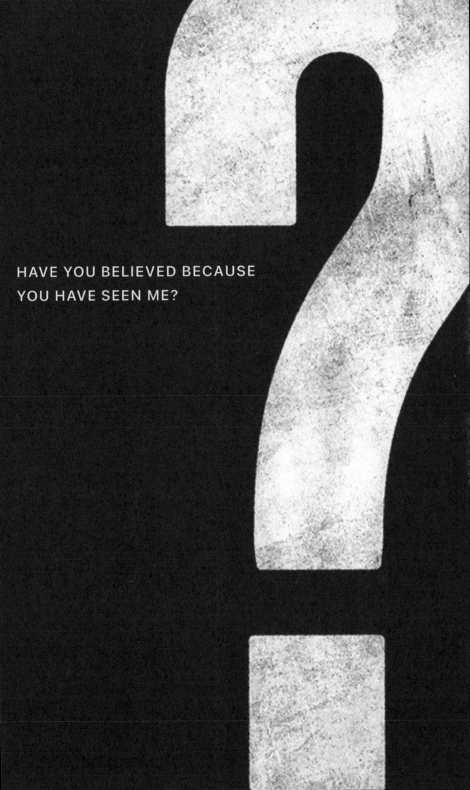

HAVE YOU BELIEVED BECAUSE
YOU HAVE SEEN ME?

4

During Times of Doubt: Jesus Shows the Way

Jesus said to him, "Have you believed because you have seen me?"

—*John 20:29*

Family vacations were a staple of my childhood. My dad had this mindset, "I work hard all year, so you better believe we're taking a vacation in the summer." As Chicagoans, one of our favorite local destinations was Wisconsin Dells, which is 150 miles away from the city. The Dells, as locals call it, is a small town with many shops, hotels, water parks, and attractions. I remember visiting Noah's Ark Waterpark, playing mini-golf at Pirate's Cove, and going to the wax museum of famous people. Another place at the Dells that always caught my attention was Ripley's Believe

It or Not! It was a museum, which founder Robert Ripley called an "odditorium," made up of weird, unique, and peculiar stories, artifacts, and photos.

Ripley was a famous cartoonist, radio host, and world traveler in the early part of the twentieth century. He made his first trip around the world in 1922, bringing back with him a collection of tales and souvenirs that sparked people's imaginations. In his lifetime Ripley collected over twenty-five thousand odd and unique artifacts and pictures that were truly unbelievable. For example, he had pictures of a Cyclops sheep, an actual elongated Peruvian skull, shrunken human heads, and photos of tribal women with rings that stretched their necks to eight inches or more. Ripley relished these oddities. He knew they were the kinds of things people wouldn't believe unless they saw it for themselves. By bringing these items back from his travels, he wanted to make the greatest skeptic into a believer of his stories. He concluded that one of the best ways to convince someone of the truthfulness of a radical story is to produce undeniable evidence—to let them see it for themselves.

Ripley's stories may reflect many of our own experiences as it pertains to the Christian faith. The resurrection of Jesus and the teachings of the Bible can be viewed by some as "believe it or not" stories. There are many people who have heard Bible stories and read the Scriptures for themselves but struggle to believe. Even if they've been raised in the church or are an active part of a church community, doubt is not uncommon for Christians.

That might be where you're at today. You may be reading this as someone who once felt strong in your faith but are now grappling with what you believe. Questions about Jesus's resurrection, the Bible's truthfulness, God's goodness or existence, and his power to change you have crept in. Perhaps that is the result of unanswered prayers, faltering health, grief, scientific discoveries, someone's abuse, or ongoing battles with sin. Maybe you've even begun to question your own salvation and relationship with God.

If that's where you're at or you feel you're heading there, God wants to meet you right at that place. On the flip side, you may not be in a space of doubt but nonetheless need your faith fortified and refortified for the ensuing battles you will face. Jesus tells his followers to "love the Lord your God with all your heart and with all your soul and with all your mind" (Matthew 22:37). It's that last phrase that often gets overlooked.

How do you love God with all your mind? The answer has everything to do with seeking to know more of who God is and what God's done. One part of the "faith seeking understanding" process is investigation.[9] In our Christian life, especially when battling doubt, it's a good thing to ask questions, just as Jesus did.

At the same time, in our question-asking, it's crucial to remember that a spiritual battle for your soul is taking place. After all, the first sin in the Bible stemmed from questions posed to Eve: "Did God actually say, 'You shall not eat of any tree in the garden'?" (Genesis 3:1). Where God wants to fortify your faith through your questions and your seeking of answers, Satan's questions work to devalue your faith and sow seeds of skepticism and distrust in God's word.

The place of wondering, questioning, and doubting can feel like a dark valley. The beauty of God's word is that it's a lamp for our feet and a light to our path (Psalm 119:105), lighting our way even in deepest valleys. In John 20, we find one of Jesus's disciples, Thomas, in a dark valley of unbelief. His experience teaches us this important lesson: the resurrected Jesus encounters people even in their doubt and questions.

Courage and Commitment

After Jesus's crucifixion and Sunday morning resurrection appearances to Mary Magdalene and the other women, Jesus reveals himself to his disciples on Sunday evening. The risen Christ showed them his hands and side (John 20:20). Instantly their hearts were filled with gladness at the sight. They were experiencing the epitome of pure joy. Jesus was crucified just days earlier for everyone in Jerusalem to see. Darkness covered the land and their hearts. They knew he had been nailed to the cross. They knew his side was pierced with a spear to confirm his death (John 19:34). Yet, he was standing in front of them alive, just as the women had told them.

This exhilarating story takes a turn when we come to John 20:24. It says, "Now Thomas, one of the Twelve, called the Twin, was not with them when Jesus came." We're not told where Thomas was, only that he wasn't there. Just imagine, of all the times to step out for a cup of coffee or run to get a gallon of milk or the one time you leave your phone in another room and you miss an important call. It's at that time that Jesus reveals himself, and Thomas missed it!

When Thomas returns, his friends announce, "We have seen the Lord." Thomas's response is what garners him the infamous nickname, "Doubting Thomas." Rattled by their joy in the face of his anguish and doubt, he says, "Unless I see in his hands the mark of the nails, and place my finger into the mark of the nails, and place my hand into his side, I will never believe" (John 20:25).

We can't blame Thomas for feeling confused and angered by their words and this missed opportunity. And if we're honest, we can hardly blame him for his skepticism. Thomas needed proof. He needed evidence of the resurrection. His faith had taken a hit on Friday and wouldn't recover so easily. Thomas didn't want hearsay. He didn't want a vision. He didn't want a hunch. Not only did he want to *see* Jesus but he wanted to *touch* Jesus.

Faith can be difficult because we long for the tangible. We want to see it. If only we could touch it, then we could more readily sift out our unbelief and enjoy the strong faith that remains. Thomas's longing for physical evidence climaxes with these words, "I will never believe." This word "never" is actually two words in the original Greek. Both are often translated as "not." Whereas in English a double negative cancels itself out, in Greek, a double negative is used for emphasis. Thomas's "I will not not believe" means "I will never" or "I will absolutely not believe."

When reading this story, we can easily forget the other things we know about Thomas aside from his doubt in this moment. Did you realize that Thomas was a man of great courage? For instance, in John 11 Jesus tells his disciples that they'll be going with him to the town of Bethany where their friend Lazarus lay dead just outside of Jerusalem. The disciples knew the religious leaders in Jerusalem hated Jesus. They had a bounty on his head. Returning to Bethany for Lazarus's funeral might result in their own funeral. As tension rose in their hearts at this thought, Thomas spoke up and "said to his fellow disciples, 'Let us also go, that we may die with him' " (John 11:16). This wasn't the result of self-destructive carelessness but of resolute determination. Thomas was bold.

Thomas was also a man of profound commitment. Like the other disciples, he left everything to follow Jesus and had no intention of turning around. In John 14 Jesus tells the disciples that he will soon depart from them, prepare a place for them, and then bring them to be with him. Jesus adds that they know the way to where he is going. Thomas is confused. How can they know the directions to the location if Jesus never gives them an address? He asks, "Lord, we do not know where you are going. How can we know the way?" (John 14:5). In these words, we not only hear a man who is thinking in very literal terms, but ultimately a man who wants to go wherever Jesus goes.

Thomas was a "ride-or-die" follower of Jesus. To use a poker term, his chips were all in. He crossed the bridge of discipleship and burned it down behind him. He wasn't turning back. And yet, he's not remembered as "ride-or-die Thomas" or "tenacious Thomas," but as "doubting Thomas."

I wonder why that is? Perhaps we remember his doubting statement most because we relate to it the most. Thomas is called "the Twin" because he likely had a twin sibling. Warren Wiersbe quips, "Who was Thomas' twin? We do not know—but sometimes you and I feel as if we might be his twins!

> Like Thomas, we all battle unbelief at different times and in different ways. For Thomas, as so often for us, deep hurt produces deep doubt and this doubt longs for compelling truth.

How often we have refused to believe and have insisted that God prove Himself to us!"[10] Like Thomas, we all battle unbelief at different times and in different ways. For Thomas, as so often for us, deep hurt produces deep doubt and this doubt longs for compelling truth.

We might expect Jesus to show up and wash away Thomas's doubt immediately. Surely Jesus will come on the scene and deliver Thomas from this battle in his faith. But that's not what Jesus does. Not even close. In John 20:26, we read, "Eight days later, his disciples were inside again, and Thomas was with them. Although the doors were locked, Jesus came and stood among them and said, 'Peace be with you.' " Did you catch that? Jesus lets Thomas linger in this place of doubt for eight days.

Eight Days Later

When counting days in the ancient world, the present day was included as day one. This means that it was now the following Sunday, a week after the resurrection when Jesus again reveals himself to the disciples. Let that sink in. Jesus waited an entire week before revealing himself to Thomas.

I wonder what kind of thoughts flooded Thomas's mind in those 168 hours that week. I wonder if he bottled up his doubt and frustration. I wonder if he became isolated in his suspicion. Did his disbelief boil over to outbursts of anger or cutting sarcasm? Did he feel ashamed of himself thinking he should "just believe" but didn't have it in him? Did he pray or could he not get himself to do so? Did he argue with his friends: "You guys must have been mistaken. You're getting your hopes up again. He's not alive"?

How do you respond when you struggle to believe in God, or his goodness, or his grace, or his forgiveness, or the truthfulness of his promises? Do you become isolated? Do you feel guilty for being where you're at? Or would you say you're numb and have a hard time feeling? Unbelief is never just a rational struggle. It affects us emotionally. It can take a toll on our lives and even our relationships.

Please understand that you're not alone. You're not the only person struggling with unbelief. And you've not been abandoned by God. Hope was on the horizon for Thomas and it's here before you.

But why did Jesus take a full week to come back around? We're given no indication that Jesus was just too busy, off doing other things. Instead, Jesus did for Thomas what he often does for us. God knows that valleys are necessary in our lives to mold our faith even in the midst of our spells of doubt. Jesus used these eight days to form Thomas. Like a steel beam heated in a fiery oven allowing it to be shaped, so God uses the struggles of life to shape and mold us to be like Jesus.

> God knows that valleys are necessary in our lives to mold our faith even in the midst of our spells of doubt.

We're told in the text that Jesus entered the room "although the doors were locked." The doors were not the only things locked that day, so was Thomas's heart. Spiritual doubt, hurt, and confusion have a way of locking up our hearts to faith. Jesus, however, has the key. The resurrected Jesus came to Thomas. His presence alone communicates, "I see you. I see your faith battle. I see your doubt. I see your struggle. Trust me, I will work those out. But I had to use this valley to do it. I will use this dark space where you can't see to teach you to grab my hand and let me lead you."

Peace Be with You

"Shalom" is a Hebrew word of greeting, a statement of favor and peace upon someone when meeting them. When seeing his disciples, Jesus says, "Peace be with you." More than a casual welcome, Jesus's words are also a pronouncement. While the disciples undoubtedly were likely terrified by this surprising appearance, the statement of "peace" addressed the anxieties of that week's events. Thomas and the others were experiencing great angst. Much like our own experience when we are confronted with the agony of doubt, anxiousness, and uncertainty about things we were once sure of, peace is the last thing we feel.

At this point, a spiritually conscious person might say Jesus was a ghost or a vision. A skeptic might say their eyes were fooling them. Some who doubt may even say that all the disciples were hallucinating.[11] These could have been the same thoughts Thomas had if this was the extent of his interaction with Jesus.

The sight of Jesus would not be sufficient to lessen Thomas's doubt. He made his conditions explicit in John 20:25, "Unless I see in his hands the mark of the nails, *and* place my finger into the mark of the nails, *and* place my hand into his side, I will never believe."[12] Jesus knew his doubt and directs the next statement to Thomas, "Put your finger here, and see my hands; and put out your hand, and place it in my side." Jesus didn't make a general statement to everyone in the room, but rather, he made a direct address to Thomas.

Jesus cares for Thomas individually. He specifically meets Thomas in his mess and unbelief. Jesus wants to do the same for you. God will speak to us in general ways and specific ways. It is important to reemphasize that God speaks through the Scriptures. In the Bible God has spoken and still speaks. Through the Scriptures he brings clarity to our uncertainties and establishes our trust. He also speaks to us specifically through the inward testimony of the Holy Spirit as we pray. He confirms the truths of his word with our hearts as the Spirit works and establishes our confidence that he is real and that we belong to him. God also uses other people as his mouthpiece. For this reason, being surrounded in a church community offers you an opportunity to be comforted by compassion, encouraged to use your gifting, refined by accountability, and built up by teaching. All of these involve the voices of other people.

That's why many people feel the Spirit move when they hear a sermon preached, sing a worship song, or listen to a prayer, feeling as if God was speaking directly to them. That's precisely what God does. He knows the battles in our hearts and wars in our minds. He knows our fight is not against flesh and blood but against the enemy of our souls and our weaknesses. God knows that. So he mercifully meets us in that place of doubt, calls us by name, and speaks to our hearts.

Just as he spoke to Thomas, he also speaks to you. In the Bible, God speaks. He actively works to uncover all kinds of lies with which you are confronted. He exposes those misleading messages that have been sown into our minds through family, popular culture, media, and entertainment. On the other hand, Satan, the enemy of our souls, uses all he can to divert us from God's truth, especially concerning the resurrection of Jesus. Without it, the entire Christian faith falters. The resurrection is God's greatest act of love for us.

Investigating the Claims

When we as God's children battle spiritual doubts and question the reality of Jesus's resurrection, we can find strength in the fact of the empty tomb. The absence of Jesus's body is a compelling defense for our faith. The eleven disciples (absent Judas Iscariot who betrayed Jesus) would not have stolen the body, manufactured a resurrection story, and then unanimously agreed on defending a lie they would end up dying for. The evidence of Mary Magdalene and the other women as the first witnesses—although their testimony would not have been accepted in a court of law—is compelling. Jesus truly died, and Jesus was truly resurrected.

> We can find strength in the fact of the empty tomb. The absence of Jesus's body is a compelling defense for our faith.

Lee Strobel was an atheist when he began investigating the reliability of the Bible and validity of Jesus's resurrection. He had a journalism degree from the University of Missouri and a law degree from Yale Law School. He was an award-winning journalist for the Chicago Tribune and other papers for fourteen years. What pushed him to investigate the Bible and empty tomb? His wife had become a Christian. So, for nearly two years, he made it his ambition to disprove the Bible. In a 2015 interview, Strobel explains what happened:

I have skepticism woven into my DNA. My knee-jerk reaction to Christianity was that it was ridiculous and not worth checking out. The idea was absurd. As I studied more in the area of atheism, I became more cemented in that view. But when my wife became a Christian and I saw positive changes in her, I decided to use my legal and journalism background to investigate it. Like one of those clown punching bags, I felt like every time I would hit Christianity with an objection, it would bounce back up.[13]

When specifically addressing the resurrection of Jesus, Strobel talks about four convincing E's. First, the *execution* of Jesus. There is no record of anyone surviving a Roman execution, so it is right to believe that Jesus had truly died.

Second, there are *early accounts* of the empty tomb, which debunks the belief that it was a myth developed over the ages. Among those accounts is the early church creed found in 1 Corinthians 15, which confesses the resurrection and was formulated within months of the empty tomb.

Third, the *empty tomb* is the most persuasive piece of them all. Jesus's opponents and those who hated his followers needed to do one simple thing to discredit their claims. All they needed to do was present Jesus's body. If they simply displayed the lifeless corpse, all of Christianity would come tumbling down. It was public knowledge where he was laid to rest. Guards were stationed at his tomb. This was no secret. And yet, they never produced the body.

Fourth, the testimonies of the many *eyewitnesses* seal the deal of resurrection evidence. There are at least nine sources from inside and outside the New Testament that testify to Jesus's resurrection.[14]

Strobel's discoveries gradually chipped away at his unbelief. On November 8, 1981 he was finally willing to attend a church service with his wife. He recalls,

> I had gone to church with Leslie that day. I can't remember anything that was said, but I came home and I just felt like after a year and nine months of looking at the evidence from science and history, and especially the resurrection, that I needed to reach a verdict. As I wrote page after page of evidence on my yellow legal pad, I just put down my pen and said, "Wait a second, it's going to take more faith to maintain my atheism than to become a Christian," because the evidence, I believed, was that strong. So that's when I concluded the resurrection was true. I read John 1:12, which says that "as many as received Him, to them He gave the right to become children of God, even to those who believe on His name." I didn't just believe it, but I repented of my sin and received His free gift of forgiveness and eternal life, and became a child of God. And my life began to change.

Strobel could no longer let his skepticism hold him back. It was time for him to let go of his resistance and fully turn to Jesus.[15]

Investigate for Yourself

There may be a host of struggles you are facing that are causing you to question your faith. Or it may be one or two things. In these times, pray a simple prayer, "God, strengthen my faith." Or you can say, "God, I'm struggling. Please help me." And then open your Bible and read. Let it wash over your doubt like ocean waves on the shore. Do this daily and journal your thoughts and prayers, entrusting yourself to God throughout your journey.

Your place of struggle may be the exclusive claims of Christianity, the historical reliability of the Bible, the evidence for the resurrection, the evidence for the deity of Jesus, the problem of evil, the difficult passages of the Bible, or reconciling God's sovereignty and our free will. Perhaps your struggles are not intellectual but a matter of the heart. You may ask one or more of the following questions: How can people who claim to follow Jesus turn a blind eye toward evils such as racism? How can spiritual leaders that I've looked up to hide a private life of deviant sinfulness and spiritual rebellion? Why am I struggling with the same sins I've prayed about for years? Why hasn't God answered my prayer for my family member's salvation?

You're not wrong for wrestling through these questions. But don't give up in your wrestling. Keep crying out to God in prayer. Keep running back to his word, meditating on passages from Psalms, Romans, or the Gospel of John. Search the Bible for answers. In addition, surround yourself with godly people who are committed to Jesus with whom

you can process your struggles, seek counsel, and be disci-
pled in a biblical perspective on the way of Jesus. Don't let
the fear of judgment hold you back. Loving God with all
your mind means that it's okay to ask questions and investigate with a heart postured toward God. Keep in mind that
God welcomes your investigation and wants to pull you in
toward himself.

Do Not Disbelieve, but Believe

In times of doubt, facts can be persuasive, but facts alone
cannot deliver us from the murky waters of cynicism into
trust in God. When Jesus encountered Thomas, he confronted him with compelling evidence—his nail-pierced
hands and his spear-punctured side—and with a radical
call to faith, "Do not disbelieve, but believe."

Jesus shows evidence and calls for a faith response. In
the moment, Jesus wants Thomas to believe he's alive and
to stop doubting. He wants to evict unbelief from his heart.
Jesus's words to Thomas are also his words to us. He wants
all of our belief. He wants us to believe he loves us so much
that he conquered death and did so to rescue us from our
mess. He wants you to put your entire faith in him.

The word "believe" occurs at least ninety-eight times
in the Gospel of John. It's an important word that is more
robust than simply a recognition of something. You can say
that you believe in the existence of a historical figure, but
by saying this, you do not mean you would put your faith
in that individual. Similarly, when John tells us to believe in

Jesus, he means more than acknowledging that Jesus existed. Jesus tells people in his own day that they see him but do not "believe" (John 6:36). Believing entails acknowledging what Jesus taught and claimed to be true (John 6:69). Believing includes embracing the truth that Jesus came to die for your sins (John 8:24). Believing leads to obeying what Jesus taught (John 8:31).

The evidence of the resurrection is before us just as the call to believe is. Will you choose to trust when some questions are answered but some questions remain? God wants us to praise him for what we do know and trust him with what we don't. Thomas had a choice in that moment to either persist in unbelief or to fully embrace Jesus, putting his spiritual wandering to rest.

My Lord and My God!

The declaration Thomas makes in John 20:28 is representative of the substance of his sincerest belief. Thomas, overwhelmed by the evidence and convinced by the truth confesses his belief in Jesus as, "My Lord and my God!" He's making a statement about his personal faith, as the pronoun "my" indicates. Thomas himself believes this. Calling Jesus "Lord" and "God" is a personal belief for Thomas, and it is directed toward Jesus.

Thomas's words echo what is written in Deuteronomy 6:4–5. It is a statement representing the core of Old Testament belief in God. It says, "Hear, O Israel: The LORD our God, the LORD is one. You shall love the LORD your

God with all your heart and with all your soul and with all your might." Thomas sees Jesus as the essence of this Scripture. He is both Lord and God of his life.

When Jesus is your Lord, he is the ruler of your life. You are his servant and he is your master. You recognize that he deserves your full submission, love, attention, and honor. You hold on to what you know to be true of him and trust in him to lead you, even when your faith feels weak.

When deep hurt creates deep doubt and deep doubt demands facts, Jesus reminds us that facts still call for faith. Jesus receives Thomas's faith confession and uses it as a teaching opportunity for his disciples that still resonates with us today.

Here Comes the Question

Let's be honest, we've all at some time thought, "If I would've lived in Bible times, I would've believed in God in a heartbeat." Aside from the fact that I think we're underestimating the stubbornness of our hearts, that sentiment also overlooks the importance of faith. Faith that requires sight really isn't faith at all. It's simply believing only in what we can see. But faith, true faith, has to do with believing things we have "not seen" (Hebrews 11:1).

Even though he needed sight to believe in the resurrection, Thomas would need a lot of faith without sight to walk the life of discipleship ahead of him. Jesus capitalizes on Thomas's experience to ask a piercing question that cuts through his demand to see. The master question-asker is at it again. Jesus examines him with these words: "Have you believed because you have seen me?" Um, yes, Thomas probably thought to himself. And that's just it. Jesus wants him to consider this. Is he only believing because he's seeing, or can he believe in Jesus even when he's not around?

Let that question sit for a moment. Change the "he" pronouns referring to Thomas to "I" pronouns referring to you. Am I only willing to believe if I can see, or can I believe in Jesus even when I can't see him physically? How would you answer Jesus's inquiry? Would you get defensive? Or would you take it in and let your heart cry out, "I believe; help my unbelief" (Mark 9:24)?

Jesus isn't looking for an answer from Thomas. He already knows it. But with his question to Thomas, he disarms his doubt and, by doing so, hands us this gift of a statement: "Blessed are those who have not seen and yet believe" (John 20:29). Everything Thomas had gone through over the past week served as a learning opportunity for him and for us. This is the kind of faith the Holy Spirit wants to cultivate in us—the faith that may not see the picture perfectly but trusts that God is in control.

But here's an important point: Christian belief may be faith without seeing, but it's not entirely blind. Because indeed, the sight we do have as part of our faith is the ability to see God's promises through the eyes of faith. We can gaze into the empty tomb with spiritual eyes and see a Savior who rose from the dead to rescue us. We can watch our Savior Jesus, who for the joy set before him endured the cross. Although we cannot see him physically, our faith is not blind!

When our eyes of faith are set upon Jesus, a life of abundant spiritual blessing follows. Jesus calls a person marked by this kind of faith the blessed one. Blessed are those who believe without seeing. They have been adopted into God's family, received forgiveness, have been declared right in God's sight, and are given the gift of the Holy Spirit to live with them. These spiritual blessings cannot be quantified in earthly riches. There's no dollar amount that can challenge its value. We cannot put a monetary price tag on forgiveness or the presence of God through the storms of life or the sure hope of the resurrection. It's true that blessed are the ones who hold on to the faith even as unbelief knocks on the front door. You can hold on to your faith because God is holding on to you.

Proof of Purchase

Whenever purchasing an item, it's a good idea to hold on to the receipt and keep it in your records. This way, if the product is defective, or doesn't function properly, and you need to get it checked out by the company, you can send it to them along with a copy of the receipt.

Like a receipt, Thomas wanted proof that Jesus was alive, and he got it. But those holes in Jesus's hands and the puncture in his side were not just proof of his resurrection, they announced to the world that anyone who puts their faith in Jesus will themselves be raised to eternal life.

You, and all who have put their faith in Jesus, are that valued product. In the beauty of God's love, he came to this earth and bought us at a high price—with his only Son's life. Even though our lives are messy, he put a value on us that transcends imagination. And whenever your faith fails, whenever you are struggling to function like you were created to, whenever you are not "working properly" and begin to wonder if God has given up on you, look to the nail-pierced hands and spear-pierced side of Jesus. These wounds are not just evidence of the fact that he defeated death and rose from the dead, but they are your proof that he loves you. They are the evidence that you belong to him. You are secure in God's hands. Your warranty never expires. Because Jesus lives, your doubt can turn into confidence. He's got you.

CHILDREN, DO YOU HAVE
ANY FISH?

5

During Times of Powerlessness: Jesus Carries Us

Children, do you have any fish?

—*John 21:5*

I 've got to admit it. My family is filled with Star Wars nerds, and I'm one of them. I'm not quite at the Comic-Con level, where fans gather at convention centers dressed up as peripheral characters only an aficionado would recognize. But I've seen all of the movies countless times and know a number of insignificant and random details. One of my favorite characters is Han Solo. In Episodes IV through VI we see his journey from being a no-good smuggler with few principles in life to becoming someone who does what is good and right. He risks his life by joining with the Rebellion (the good guys) to overthrow the Empire (the bad guys). He and his strong furry friend Chewbacca become heroes for their bravery and commitment.

However, when *Episode VII: The Force Awakens* was released in 2015, fans were shocked to see what had become of him. In the thirty years that passed in the storyline, we see Han Solo no longer with the Rebellion but back in the smuggling business. He's making a living off cheating dangerous people and lying to get himself out of precarious situations. Solo and Chewbacca are a far cry from the heroes we saw in the previous movies. What changed? Failure. In those thirty years, Han Solo failed as a father and husband, and he retreated to what he was familiar with, even if it wasn't the right thing to do.

Failure is messy. It can cause even the best of us to lose focus, to fall back to our old ways, or just to feel stuck. Our default mode is to pursue comfort, familiarity, and self-preservation. But these often don't align with what God wants for us. You may sense God moving you in a new career direction, but the last time you tried to step out in faith, things didn't go so well, so you stay put. You may sense God calling you to persevere and serve faithfully where you're at, but the unknowns and potential for failure causes you to uproot to somewhere safer, smoother, and more attractive.

Think about a time you strove to be radical in your obedience to God and did something bold. For example, the time you said yes to a ministry opportunity, the time you spoke up about your faith, or the time you poured your life into caring for someone. Things felt good and right in those moments and seasons. But what happened after you stepped out and then stumbled? After you spoke up but lost your cool? After you agreed to an opportunity and then felt you made the wrong decision? After you invested time pouring your life into someone and then they strayed from the faith? What did you do when things didn't pan out the way you hoped or when you flat out failed? Whether in small ways or large ones, at the point of failure or at the point of difficulty, many Christians fall.

Like everyone, followers of Jesus at times return to their old ways or retreat to places of ease when they've experienced a letdown rather than pressing on with courageous resolve. We become discouraged, ashamed, or disappointed with ourselves. The fruit of confusion is feeling lost, a sense of wandering without purpose. In those moments, we need to understand that even though God's plan may not seem clear to us, it's clear to God.

> Even though God's plan may not seem clear to us, it's clear to God.

There are lessons God wants to teach us even in our failures, flops, and wanderings—even in our messes.

The True Vine

The night of Jesus's betrayal he gave the disciples an illustration of him as a vine and his followers as the branches connected to the vine. Branches attached to the vine can bear fruit, such as grapes. However, once a branch is cut off, it no longer has the capability of growing fruit on its own.

With that, Jesus says, "Apart from me you can do nothing" (John 15:5). He wants his disciples then, and his disciples now, to understand that life without Jesus is fruitless. Life without Jesus is purposeless. Life without Jesus is powerless. Jesus knew his disciples needed to hear this. After all, his crucifixion was only hours away.

The disciples heard Jesus speak these words on Thursday night and just hours later he was bitterly betrayed, secretly arrested, falsely accused, illegally tried, wrongfully condemned, maliciously beaten, and mercilessly crucified. The disciples fled—all of them. For three days they wandered in fearful confusion. Then came Sunday morning when Jesus's disciples witnessed his glorious resurrection three days after they witnessed his death. What would these emotionally jarred disciples do after the resurrection? On the horizon for the disciples was a personal lesson on dependency upon God.

It had been over a week since Jesus walked out of the grave, and the disciples went north to Galilee as he instructed them. This is the context for John 21:1–14 where we find seven disciples—Peter, Thomas, Nathanael, James, John, and two others—reemerge into the story on the shores of the Sea of Galilee. While they knew that Jesus had conquered death, they were fishing on a boat without direction and without power.

Before we look at Jesus's encounter with them, let's take a closer look at these specific disciples. Peter was a fisherman known for his bold declarations and prominence among the disciples. Thomas was the one who struggled with unbelief and lingered in it for a week before he saw the risen Lord. This is Nathanael's second appearance in the Gospel of John. When we first meet him, Nathanael utters the infamous words, "Can anything good come out of Nazareth?" (John 1:46). Then Jesus gives him information about himself that only someone who had access to divine insight could know. Nathanael should've asked, *Can anything good come out of me?*

The next disciples mentioned are the sons of Zebedee and two others. While we can only speculate about the identity of the two "other" disciples, we can be certain that Zebedee's sons were James and John. They were friends of Peter and fellow fishermen who spent countless hours on the Sea of Galilee. That is, before encountering Jesus.

Earlier, in Luke 5:1–11, Jesus finds Peter with James and John while cleaning their fishing equipment after a night of catching nothing. Jesus sees their failure as an opportunity and tells Peter to get back into the boat and cast his net into the sea. Reluctantly, Peter lets down his net and hauls in an astonishing catch. The sons of Zebedee witnessed this firsthand and were amazed. These fishermen learned that with Jesus all things were possible. Peter is broken by his unbelief, and it's hard to imagine that James and John were not equally embarrassed. At that moment, Jesus speaks his calling over them: "Do not be afraid," he said, "from now on you will be catching men" (Luke 5:10).

Jesus planned for James, John, and Peter to carry the message of his salvation to people. Through these men, God would snatch up people who were headed to destruction and give them new lives. When Zebedee's sons and Peter returned to land, they left everything to follow Jesus. He became their rabbi (teacher) and they became his disciples. These fishermen would become fishers of men. Fishing as a calling was now a thing of their past. Or was it?

"I'm Going Fishing"

These seven men are the ones that Jesus visits as the John 21 story develops. Thomas, Nathanael, James, John, and the two others were with Peter on that day over a week after the resurrection. Peter invites the men to join him on a boat in John 21:2 when he says, "I am going fishing." At first glance, we simply see a man who is enjoying a hobby with friends or trying to catch dinner for the family. And yet, there is likely more to the scene. The next verse tells us that they fished all night and caught nothing. Sound familiar? The last time a failed night of fishing is recorded in the New Testament is right before Jesus called Peter, James, and John to follow him. It's a parallel scene from several of their lives before they started following Jesus.

Could it be that failure caused them to retreat to what was comfortable? Could it be that they resorted to what was familiar when they were uncertain what to do? Could it be that there was waning purpose in their lives? It's very likely. There's no indication that they completely strayed away from Jesus. We know they were in the Galilee region precisely because Jesus told them to meet him there (Matthew 28:7).

But it does appear that they lacked something important: purpose and power. Their unsuccessful night prepared the way for them to learn a critical lesson before embarking on their soon-to-be new mission.

As the narrative unfolds, it is not far-fetched to see that confusion, regret, or aimlessness played a significant role in their retreating. Suddenly, this oddly detailed narrative becomes highly applicable. We are no one to judge. It is our same impulse to return to what "worked" when the risks we take don't pan out. We've been in the same boat, floating about, when we're dejected. Following Jesus was risky, and things did not turn out the way they had anticipated. In the normal routines of life, going back to what worked may not always be a bad decision. For example, if you try a new fitness routine but it's not producing the results an old routine did, it makes sense to go back to what worked. In the Christian life, however, returning to a way of life that is driven by fear or fails to place Jesus at the center is always catastrophic.

Returning to What We Know

Have your sinful choices or failures to walk with Jesus caused you to retreat to what is familiar? Do you find yourself tempted to return to what was "comfortable" out of either fear of failing again or out of feeling unredeemable? People have told me, "Life seemed easier when I wasn't following Jesus. I didn't feel spiritual attack like I do now." And they look back on "those days" wondering if that comfort is worth returning to. These lines of thinking are not new. In 1616 the English pastor William Gouge addressed this idea of feeling less spiritual attack when a Christian is not pursuing Jesus. "I easily believe it," he says, adding that because the devil already has them in his power, he has no need to pursue them.[16] Spiritually speaking, what is comfortable does not necessarily equate to being in a "good place."

Another clear tactic of Satan is to provoke us into believing that sin has disqualified us from making a kingdom impact. Rather than seeing our failure as an opportunity to let God's transforming grace be placed on display through forgiving us and restoring us, we let shame persuade us to flee. We consign ourselves to backsliding rather than choosing to step forward.

Peter hopped back on the boat and brought the other six men with him. What boats are you jumping back onto? Has God delivered you from alcoholism, but your sin has brought you back to the bottle? Has God freed you from a toxic relationship, but your disobedience leads you to flirt with it again? Has God freed you from the love of money, but you suppress your feeling of guilt over your sin by working more hours and making more money? Peter's shame took him back to a boat.

Let's be clear, there is nothing inherently wrong with fishing. This is not about their vocation as much as it is about their calling. For each of the seven disciples present, their calling as disciples and preachers of the gospel influenced their vocation, but the calling was the important piece. This is the case for you and me. Whether you're a machinist, mail carrier, homemaker, baker, salesman, real estate agent, rideshare driver, small business owner, engineer, educator, or police officer by vocation, *what* you do is not as important as *how* you do it. Let your calling as a follower of Jesus so influence your life that you do everything with a view of bringing God glory and causing the

> Do everything with a view of bringing God glory and causing the aroma of Christ to follow you everywhere you go. That's purposeful (and not aimless) living.

aroma of Christ to follow you everywhere you go. That's purposeful (and not aimless) living.

Still there may be some, like these seven disciples, who through their calling receive a new vocation. Perhaps God moves you away from one field to bring you to another to represent him in ways unique to your gifts. He may call you to leave your sales profession to become an overseas missionary. He may lead you to sell your business to enter pastoral ministry. Whatever the case is, know your calling as a follower of Jesus and let neither fear nor failure prevent you from living that out.

There's no definitive indication in the text that these men were in gross rebellion. However, the description and narrative flow seem to indicate that they were lacking something. This aspect of the story is undeniable: "Their efforts were in vain."[17] D. A. Carson puts it this way, "They are coming to grips with the resurrection, but they still have not learned the profound truth that apart from Christ they can do noth-ing."[18] That's precisely what that night of fishing symbolized. They caught nothing without Jesus on the Sea of Galilee just as they can do nothing apart from him in all of life.

How's that Working for You?

At daybreak, as the seven fishermen approached the shore from their boats empty-handed, they were greeted by a voice in the distance. The man didn't say hello, but instead asked them a perfectly placed question. "Do you have any fish?" Ouch! This was the kind of question that could fur-ther frustrate any unsuccessful crew. The inquisitive man on the shore was no novice question-asker. He was a seasoned veteran. It was Jesus.

Like a boxer who throws a jab after the bell, this ques-tion may have felt like a cheap shot. But we know Jesus. We know he's neither vindictive nor vicious. Yet, we also know he won't coddle emotions when we need an adjustment. His question was pregnant with meaning. He wasn't asking for a numerical figure but asking in order to expose their motives and point out their fruitless night. In essence, Jesus asked, "Hey guys, how's going back to your old ways working for you?" The clear answer? Not so good.

When failure and purposelessness push us to retreat, we're not in a good place. In fact, we're in a terrible place. Isolation from God is devastation for the heart. Satan prefers our wandering, so long as we don't turn to Jesus. The evil one wants to isolate God's people from the refuge of God's grace. When we drift, we are in danger.

When Adam and Eve ate the fruit in the garden of Eden, their eyes were opened to the realities of good and evil, life and death. This revelation and its subsequent guilt were beyond what they could process. They tried to cover their failure with fig leaves, and they hid. But from whom did Adam and Eve hide themselves? They were literally the only ones on the earth! They hid themselves from God. They dodged the very one they needed most in that moment. How tempting it is to follow in their footsteps. Like Adam and Eve, we can become so ashamed of ourselves and crushed by our actions that we try to cover our failures and hide ourselves. We stop staying in contact with our friends who love Jesus. We slowly disconnect from the church community. We pray less frequently and open our Bible periodically. In our culpability we become isolated, vulnerable, and exposed to our own way of thinking.

Jesus knew about the disciples' catch. Or lack thereof. He knew their nets were empty. Yet, even though Jesus knew it, he still asks them this frustrating question. Why? Because he wants them to acknowledge their emptiness so that healing can take place. Until we swallow our pride and acknowledge our emptiness, there's no space for Jesus in our lives. It's like God has a U-Haul truck filled with grace and mercy ready to be poured out, but until we acknowledge we need it, it stays double-parked at the curb of our hearts.

We don't need to pretend everything is okay. We can stop
running to our old ways of doing things. We can cease drifting from one place to the next. Sure, life is messy right now.
Sure, you've failed. But any impulse or message that floats
around in your mind that says you can't come to God with
your mess, failure, or misdirection is not a message from the
Holy Spirit. It's not from God. Instead, God invites you and
me—weary sailors, haggard from drifting—to come to him.
If you find yourself at your wit's end, why not return to him?

With Jesus, Anything Is Possible

Jesus was still hidden from the fishermen's recognition. It
was time for them to understand that *apart from Jesus* they
can do nothing. Or to put it another way, it was time for
them to see that *with Jesus* they can do anything. At daybreak
Jesus shouts to them to cast their nets to the right side of the
boat. Apart from the Lord, this is nonsense, but with Jesus,
the impossible becomes possible. And so, they cast their
nets and reel in 153 fish! Jesus was there to show them a
better way—the way of walking in step with him even when
things don't seem possible or when things hadn't previously
worked out. Rather than leaning on our own understanding, we need to trust in Jesus. Do what he says. Follow him.

The "disciple whom Jesus loved" is a codename for
John the son of Zebedee when he writes about himself in
this Gospel. He's the first one to recognize the identity of
Jesus and tells Peter, "It is the Lord!" Though sorrow and

disappointment may last for the night, joy comes in the morning. Peter jumps into the lake and swims over to Jesus. They all come to shore and eat breakfast with their redeemer and teacher.

Jesus was alive. He was truly there in human flesh having come up out from the grave. It was the third time they had seen their resurrected Savior after his crucifixion. The fish he ate didn't fall through his mouth and body onto the floor as if he were a spirit. He didn't disappear from their sight when they blinked their eyes as if he were a vision. His words were not construed differently as if the voice was in their collective imagination. His invitation to "come and have breakfast" was not made up, as if he didn't defeat death. No, he's there in bodily form. And because he's alive, they learn that with Jesus anything is possible. New beginnings are available. Getting up after falling down can happen. Living with power and purpose is a reality.

While it is true that we can't do anything of eternal impact apart from Jesus, it's also true that Jesus chooses to do something through us. He doesn't need us. He doesn't have to use us. He didn't need them to cast their nets. He could have had 153 fish jump into their boat without them casting their nets just as easily as he had the fish jump into their nets *after* they cast them. Jesus's actions invited the disciples to act. Jesus allowed the disciples to participate in what he was doing. Not only does he graciously give hope, he also infuses us with purpose.

Like Cutting Squash

When my youngest son Levi was eight years old, he enjoyed helping around the kitchen. One evening he helped me cut squash in preparation for a soup Erikah was making. Squash has a hard outer shell, and our kitchen knives were not the best, which made cutting it difficult for an adult, let alone an eight-year-old boy. When he asked to help, I immediately realized that this would be faster and easier if I just did it myself. But I also recognized how badly Levi wanted to help. I gave him the knife and showed him how to make the cuts. As I expected, he wasn't able to do it. He simply didn't have the strength to get through the shell. In some ways, I wanted to thank him for trying and take over, but then I would have missed an opportunity for him to learn and participate. So, I stood behind him, put my palm on top of his hand that held the knife, and gently applied some force. As he cut in a downward motion the knife penetrated the solid squash shell. We did this several times to make cubed pieces, and it put a huge smile on Levi's face. Even though he couldn't do it by himself, he was glad to be a part of it. On my part, I was happy for him. I could see the thrill on his face that he helped make dinner. In my impatience, I almost missed out on his excitement and the spiritual lesson I learned through it.

We all lack the strength to lead lives of eternal impact. On our own, we lack what it takes to stand up when we fall and to walk with purpose and power. Our efforts, removed from Jesus, are in vain. But God delights in meeting us in our weaknesses. He doesn't shove us out of the way and say he's through with us. Rather, as a gentle Savior, he covers our hands with his and applies his strength to our weaknesses. He chooses to allow us to participate so we can experience the thrill of seeing God move through us. God doesn't need our help, but he delights in using us to accomplish his will. Jesus's teaching that "apart from me you can do nothing" doesn't mean he wants you to do nothing. No! He wants you to live with purpose, on mission, with his strength. And he wants you to know you need him to do it.

Years ago, I received an opportunity to preach at a large conference. I was genuinely humbled by the request, excited to preach, and terrified by the size of the audience that would listen in through a variety of platforms. It was humbling to receive the request because I had been personally shaped by this conference in previous years as an attendee. And, of course, I was thrilled to preach. To me, preaching is the result of God putting a fire in my bones that I can't keep in (Jeremiah 20:9). But I was terrified. In my purest struggles, I felt the onus of so many listening and wanted to be a good steward of the opportunity and faithful to God with the biblical text and my words. In my impure struggles, I wanted people to like me. I felt the weight of spiritual attack and began to grow anxious as the days got closer. The night before I was to preach, I felt such an awful weight on my soul that I thought I was going to have a panic attack. I even considered scrapping my entire sermon and preaching something different twelve hours before. Looking back, I can see areas where I faltered. I hadn't prayed like I needed to. I let my fear of man overtake my fear of God. I jumped back into my old boat of self-reliance and selfish ambition, and I became a mess.

As I processed my anxiety with my wife the night before the sermon, she reminded me of God's character and his calling over my life, and she allowed me to verbally process my fears. I didn't have what it took to pull myself together. I didn't have what was needed to get up and preach the next day. But God did. Through my repentant heart, he placed his hand on me and applied his strength to my weakness. Late that night I experienced God's peace. When you're confident in God's character, you can rest in his will. Our God is faithful and loves his people far more than I could ever love them. Apart from him I could do nothing, but with him I was able to preach the next day and point many people to Jesus.

> When you're confident in God's character, you can rest in his will. Our God is faithful and loves his people far more than I could ever love them.

They Got It

This incident on the sea prepared these seven disciples for what God would do through them in the years to come. On the day of Pentecost, fifty days after Jesus's resurrection, the Holy Spirit fell upon them in power as they talked about God's wonderful works and the salvation he offers in Jesus (Acts 2:1–11). With Jesus and the empowerment of the Holy Spirit, they could do anything. In Jesus's name Peter and John healed a paralytic and boldly shared the good news of Jesus even while under arrest for the message (Acts 3:1–10; 4:1–3). In the name of Jesus all things are possible. Again, the "apostles"—a title that undoubtedly included several of the seven who were on the Sea of Galilee in John 21—were arrested for preaching Jesus but refused to stop. They told their persecutors, "We must obey God rather than men" (Acts 5:29) and rejoiced in the midst of their suffering (5:40–42). The power of God was visibly at work in men who could do nothing without him. James the son of Zebedee stood courageously in his faith to the point of execution at the hands of Herod (Acts 12:2). John, the other son of Zebedee, spent his dying days exiled on the prison island of Patmos after a life lived in faithfulness to his Savior (Revelation 1:9). Apart from Jesus the disciples could do nothing, but with Jesus they could do anything in alignment with God's will.

History shows they got it. They understood the lesson they needed to learn on the Sea of Galilee that day when the resurrected Jesus met them in their mess. Going back to the boat and a night of fruitless fishing taught them that life without Jesus is as empty as their nets and directionless as drifting on the sea. But in Jesus's power and commissioning, they would be his missionaries casting gospel nets throughout the Roman Empire.

My prayer is that you would see how Jesus can and will meet you in the mess of wanting to go back to your previous life or old ways of thinking. I pray you would see that the resurrected Jesus can and will guide you in his purpose and place you in his mission when you are aimless and faltering. Sometimes the most difficult mess we find ourselves in is feeling stuck. Here's the good news. While apart from Jesus, you can do nothing, but with Jesus all things are possible. Because he lives, our powerless drifting can turn into an empowered purpose.

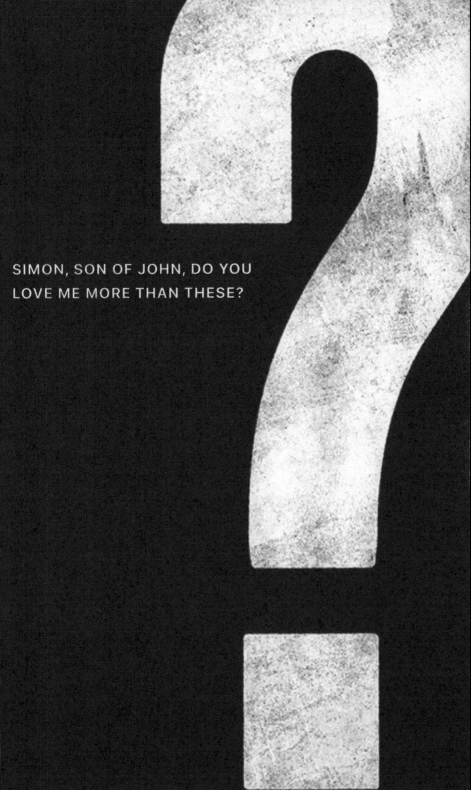

SIMON, SON OF JOHN, DO YOU
LOVE ME MORE THAN THESE?

6

When You Make Mistakes: Jesus Forgives

Jesus said to Simon Peter, "Simon, son of John, do you love me more than these?"

—*John 21:15*

Several years ago, I came across the remarkable story of a twenty-year-old Christian man named Vincent Jukes born around 1618.[19] As a young adult he went to culinary school and got a job as a chef aboard a ship sailing from England to Italy. While at sea, pirates spotted the vessel and overtook it. Seven voyagers onboard Jukes's boat were killed and another twenty wounded. Jukes and thirty-three others were now prisoners on their own ship. The boat was rerouted to Algiers in North Africa where they were sold as slaves. Jukes was purchased by a slaveowner who repeatedly beat him and wanted him to renounce his faith in Jesus. Under these attacks, Jukes caved in and abandoned Jesus, denying his Savior. This was his way of life for nearly two years.

In early 1638, Jukes seized an opportunity to run away to Spain, and in April of that year he returned to England. But he now had a secret. No one knew he had renounced his faith under persecution. Only Jukes knew that he denied Christ. It was a truth he tried to keep secret, but one day he couldn't any more. Convicted by his sin, he confessed to a spiritual adviser that he had verbally abandoned his faith in Jesus under the threat of injury. Jukes wondered, "Can God forgive me for turning my back on him? Is it over for me?"

Though with differing circumstances, this is a painful question you may have whispered softly in your mind or even uttered with your lips. Our sin puts us in a place of spiritual isolation. It's as if, like a football running back to a defender, we give God the stiff-arm. We leap over the Spirit's warnings to not proceed and sprint into our rebellion. And when we come to our senses after sinning against God, we are bombarded with a host of regretful emotions and painful questions. Why did I do this? What was I thinking? How did I get here? Is there any hope left for me? Is God done with me? My life is a mess. Can I ever again be whole?

An Infamous Failure

Few people in the Bible are known as equally by their remarkable successes as they are by their embarrassing failures as the apostle Peter. His story is endeared to many Christians because we can see something of ourselves in his life. He had courage. He was assertive. He had flashes of astonishing faith. His boldness is infectious. Yet, he has moments of dramatic failure. He puts his foot in his mouth. He writes checks with his words that his actions can't cash. He makes promises that he's incapable of delivering. He's like you and me. He was a person who loved Jesus and whose life was messy.

Peter's greatest failure is well-documented and eerily famous. He's the guy who denied Jesus. He's the one who, out of fear, swore he didn't know Jesus hours before Jesus was crucified. That Peter. That's the one I'm talking about.

It was late Thursday night when Jesus shared the Passover meal with his disciples. He taught them what is known as "the upper room discourse." It was a kind of "last words" sermon from Jesus to his disciples. They didn't know what was on the horizon. Jesus plainly stated that he would be arrested and killed, but it didn't register with them. With his crucifixion in mind, Jesus told Peter and the other disciples that they couldn't join him in the place he was about to go. Peter boldly responds, "Lord, why can I not follow you now? I will lay down my life for you" (John 13:38). Jesus raises the stakes and says that all of them will run away from him. They won't be there for him at his greatest time of need. Even worse, Peter himself would deny Jesus three times before the rooster crows twice that morning. Peter, offended by these words, retorts, "Even though they all fall

away, I will not. ... If I must die with you, I will not deny
you" (Mark 14:26–31).

Peter loved Jesus with devoted sincerity. While he was
aware of his own imperfections, he couldn't fathom ever
walking away from Jesus or denying him in any way. After
all, it was Peter who earlier had confessed Jesus to be the
Savior of the world. Hours later, before dawn on Friday
morning, a band of soldiers authorized by the chief priest
apprehended Jesus. Peter famously pulls out his sword and
strikes a soldier's ear, but moments later, he runs away like
the rest of Jesus's friends. They left Jesus alone as he was
taken into custody. However, Peter followed "at a distance"
(Luke 22:54). This weary disciple entered the high priest's
courtyard and warmed himself by a fire.

But Peter couldn't hide his identity. He was recognized
almost immediately by several people around the fire, and
they began to question him. They essentially asked, "Aren't
you one of his disciples? Didn't I see you in the garden when
we arrested Jesus?" Three times Peter was questioned and
three times Peter denied Jesus. Desperately desiring to be
persuasive, Peter invokes a curse upon himself to make his
point: "A curse on me if I'm lying—I don't know this man
you're talking about!" (Mark 14:71 NLT).[20]

Across the courtyard, Jesus's eyes locked onto Peter's
(Luke 22:61). Instant regret and pain ensued. Jesus had been
there for Peter whenever he needed him. Peter couldn't
return the favor. He'd failed. He'd deserted Jesus with his
actions and his words. Peter's emotions gripped him and

all he could do was weep. These weren't merely tears of sadness. These were tears of bitter regret. Tears of shame. These are the kinds of tears we cry when we wish we could undo something we have just done.

It was over for Peter. How could he ever look Jesus in the eye again? Even worse, Jesus now faced execution. In Peter's mind, God was done with him. And he was done with himself. His world came crashing down, and he chipped away at his own foundation. He pulled out the Jenga block that collapsed the whole tower of his life. His life was a mess because of his own cowardice. He had no one to blame but himself. No doubt, Peter asked himself, "How did I get here?"

How Did I Get Here?

One compromise can change everything. But one compromise results from a line of previous choices. As Christian rap artist Da' T.R.U.T.H. says of sin and compromise,

It wasn't all of a sudden it was subtle
    What ended up as a flood started out as a puddle
Yeah, I should have stayed in the huddle
    And I never should have let my hair down like
    Rapunzel[21]

Too often we negotiate with sin like buying clothing from a street vender. We go after what we want but try to minimize the cost in the process. Sin is subtle. It lurks in our hearts and is never fully satisfied.

The Bible tells us to "give no opportunity to the devil" (Ephesians 4:27) and to "not be outwitted by Satan" nor to be "ignorant of his designs" (2 Corinthians 2:11). Satan wants to appeal to our sinful nature and weaken the footing of our faith. With each concession we give, our foundation erodes, and denying Jesus with our words or by our lives becomes a consistent possibility and struggle.

A drug addiction can begin with an escape to a "smaller" substance. A sexual affair can begin with an unchecked lustful glance. Habitual dishonesty can start out as a "white lie" or "exaggeration" for the sake of self-preservation. A destructive outburst of rage may begin with simmering hate. Cold denials of Jesus can start from a pattern of neglected prayer, Bible reading, or community worship. These are puddles that lead to floods.

Chicago is a great city. In my biased opinion, it's the best. Our sports teams are iconic: White Sox, Bulls, Bears, Blackhawks, and Cubs. Our athletes are historic: Michael Jordan, Scottie Pippen, Walter Payton, Frank Thomas, Ernie Banks, Patrick Kane. Our attractions are legendary: Sears Tower, Magnificent Mile, Field Museum, Navy Pier, Millennium Park, the Bean.[22] Our food is unforgettable: Chicago deep-dish pizza, Chicago-style hot dog, the jibarito Puerto Rican sandwich, Italian beef, signature steak. This being said, there's plenty to not like about the city as well. Our "windy" politics, extreme taxes, high cost of living, segregated communities, and crime are regular frustrations. But one of the worst things is something in which we perennially lead the nation. Check out this 2020 headline: "Chicago Named 'Rattiest City' in America for 6th Year in a Row."[23]

That's us. The nation's most rat-infested city. The Chicago restaurant industry, densely populated neighborhoods, and back alleys where the trash is kept provide the perfect breeding ground for these rodents. Orkin pest-control service entomologist Ben Hottel says, "Rodents are experts at sniffing out food and shelter, and they're resilient in their ways to obtain both." He continues, "Residential properties offer the ideal habitat for rodents, and once they've settled in, they're capable of reproducing rapidly and in large quantities."[24] It turns out, rodents and sin have a lot in common. Sin can begin with a small compromise but take over your "home" in no time. It's resilient. It reproduces quickly, and when we're living under the influence of our fleshly nature, it reveals itself in large ways through our lives.

None of us would willfully leave our back door cracked open with a mischief of rats hanging out on the porch. But that's what we do with sin when we let our spiritual guard down by keeping the door open and flirting with temptation. That was what happened to Peter.

The night of Jesus's arrest, the Bible tells us that Peter's spirit was willing but his flesh was weak. Deep down inside he wanted to do what was right, but outwardly his will was weakened by the circumstances around him. As his Savior prayed in the garden of Gethsemane, Peter slept (Matthew 26:40). Exhaustion won over fervency. Fatigue let his guard down, and when it came time for the battle, he dropped the sword of the Spirit and unsheathed the sword of his flesh. He walked by sight and not by faith. Just as you can't eradicate an infestation of rats with some steel wool and a few traps, we can't exterminate sin with our best efforts. We need God and we need him badly.

He Left Everything

As Peter wept in that smoky courtyard, I wonder if his mind flashed back to the day he met Jesus. Peter and several of the other disciples were fishermen by trade. After an unsuccessful night of fishing, Jesus approached Peter on the shores of the Sea of Galilee (Luke 5:1–11). He asked Peter if he could use his boat as a platform from which to teach. If Jesus were to sit on the boat a little from shore, his voice could travel over the water and the shore would function like a megaphone. Peter welcomed the request.

After teaching, Jesus directed Peter to take the boat and his freshly washed net out into the deep and give fishing another go. Peter was exasperated by the request. Fishermen don't do this. They don't dirty their nets after cleaning them. They don't take fishing instructions from a rabbi. They don't cast a net for fish when the fish aren't biting.[25] But Peter, respecting Jesus as his master, concedes. The moment his crew lets down their nets fish began to fill them. The fishermen were overwhelmed, and Peter was embarrassed. "Depart from me, for I am a sinful man," he confessed.

Jesus didn't just salvage the situation; he orchestrated it. He told Peter with irresistible persuasion, "From now on you will be catching men." Peter left everything and followed Jesus, only to quickly find out that he gained everything at the same time.

Fast forward three years later. With three exposing questions, followed by three bold statements and two rooster crows, Peter left Jesus and seemingly lost everything. That is, everything that truly mattered.

When we give in to sin, it can feel as if all that was good in life fell apart in a moment. We may even wonder, "Can what has been broken ever be put back together again? Is everything lost?"

This Rock

When Peter left the scene of his denial, I wonder if he recalled the day Jesus gave him the name Peter. He was, after all, Simon by birth. But by now, everyone knew him as Simon Peter. The name Peter in Greek is *petros,* which means "rock."[26] Peter was the Rock long before actor Dwayne Johnson. The title "Rock" is a nickname that implies a person is sturdy, strong, and immovable. This was descriptive of the faith and perseverance Jesus would build in Peter.

One day while Jesus conversed with his disciples, Peter made a memorable affirmation regarding Jesus's identity. He confessed Jesus was indeed the Anointed One, the Deliverer, the long-awaited Messiah—the Christ that has come from God. Amplifying the symbolism of the name change, Jesus told Peter, "You are Peter, and upon this rock I will build my church" (Matthew 16:18). Jesus wanted Peter, along with the other eleven disciples, to carry the mantle when he left. These were the people God would use to build his church and advance the good news of the empty tomb.

However, the title "Rock" hardly describes the Peter we see that fateful night of Jesus's betrayal. He's not a man who's sturdy, but a man who is confused. He's not strong, but quite weak. He is unreliable, not immovable. He's not a rock. He's a bowl of Jell-O, easily shaken and influenced by everything around him.

I can imagine Peter with his fists clenched, screaming within. Enraged by his weakness and mortified by his denial, did Peter remember the other thing Jesus shared with him the night before? When Jesus told Peter he would deny him three times, he also said something else. He pulled back the curtain between the ordinary world as we see it and the spiritual world around us. Jesus gave Peter a glimpse into that realm: "Simon, Simon, behold, Satan demanded to have you, that he might sift you like wheat," said Jesus. "But I have prayed for you that your faith may not fail" (Luke 22:31–32).

But his faith did fail. From all vantage points, it appeared that Satan had won. Peter was defeated. Was it over for him? He seemed to think so. That very day Jesus was publicly crucified, and Peter was nowhere to be found.

"Do You Love Me?"

The mess of Peter's life was too great. Regret had him locked down. By this point, Peter had experienced Jesus's resurrection but did not believe that Jesus could resurrect him.

God can redeem our greatest failures and work something marvelous from it. He is like a master sculptor molding less-than-ideal clay into priceless treasures. Jesus gave Peter the name Rock and promised "upon this rock I will build my church." Little did Peter know that he, "the rock," would hit rock bottom. But as preacher and scholar Tony Evans says, "Sometimes God lets you hit rock bottom so that you will discover that He is the Rock at the bottom."[27]

Sin had Peter in a straitjacket—tied up with regret. Jesus knew it. Jesus understood the power of sin. After all, he had just taken the world's transgressions all the way to the grave. Because he loves us, Jesus embraced the cross and tomb to take on our unparalleled foe and trample him beneath his feet. As William Branch sings, "Sin's got the lock, but God's got the key!"[28]

In order for a key to open a lock, it has to get inside it to access the bolt. We've all gone through the experience of grabbing a key from our keychain and putting it into a lock only to realize we have a *similar* key in hand but not the *exact* one for the lock. That's why color coding keys can be helpful. A similar key may fit into the lock, but it cannot turn it. It feels like it should work, but it doesn't. The same is true of freedom from our bondage to sin. We may try things in our lives that seem to get us close to freedom from sin, shame, and guilt, but they don't quite deliver.

Jesus, however, is the real deal. He is the key. He entered Peter's heart to unlock his guilt through his favorite strategy—questions. Over a week after his resurrection, Jesus met

Peter and six other disciples on the shores of the Sea of Galilee. In John 21 he brought new meaning to their unsuccessful night of fishing with a question, and then he went on a walk with Peter, breaching his heart the same way. In John 21:15 Jesus asks Peter, "Simon, son of John, do you love me more than these?" The last time Jesus called Peter by his birth name along with his father's name was when Jesus gave him the new appellation "Peter." With this subtle, yet intentional choice, Jesus is reminding Peter of whom he has called him to be. When Jesus gave Peter the moniker Rock, he wasn't giving a prediction but making a declaration. Here, on the shores of the Sea of Galilee, Jesus had every intention of restoring to Peter this identity. But it would take a painful conversation to release him from the manacles of guilt.

Jesus asked Peter, "Do you love me?" But Jesus's question didn't stop there. He asks, "Do you love me *more than these*?" Biblical scholars dispute to whom or what "these" refers. The question narrows down to two possibilities. One option is that Jesus asks if Peter loves him more than these other disciples standing near them. The other option is that Peter loves Jesus more than the fishing boat and net. In either case, Jesus questions Peter's love. Peter had left the familiarity of the Galilean sea to plunge into the depths of following Jesus. Peter had to spends days and weeks away from his wife. People undoubtedly jeered at his negligence—leaving his family to follow a Nazareth-born, self-proclaimed rabbi of no repute. Of course, Peter loved Jesus. But how do we explain Peter's fierce denial of Christ? What do we make of his insistence that he did not know Jesus? Those are not the words nor actions of one who loves someone, are they?

Jesus's question called to mind both the way Peter boasted of his devotion to Jesus after the Last Supper and the three times Peter denied Jesus hours after that. Peter's actions on Good Friday justifiably cast a shadow of doubt over his love for Jesus. After all, Jesus said in John 14:15, "If you love me, you will keep my commandments." Denying Jesus is rejecting Jesus. Even if it was out of the fear of man or self-preservation, Peter sinned against God and turned his back on his Lord.

The inquiry may have felt like an interrogation, but Peter responds, "Yes, Lord; you know that I love you." Peter's confession is followed by Jesus giving him this imperative: "Feed my lambs." With the utterance of these words Jesus recommissions Peter, essentially telling him, "Peter, you've got work to do. I need you to be like a shepherd and feed my sheep—my followers."

This first exchange wasn't enough for Jesus. He goes through the same sequence of questions and statements with Peter two more times. [29] By the third time Jesus asked Peter if he loved him, the writer says that Peter was "grieved." Peter's response exhibits this pain, "Lord, you know everything; you know that I love you." Peter acknowledges Jesus's omniscience. It's as if Peter is saying, "Jesus, nothing can escape your knowledge. Before you, I am naked and exposed. You see my pain and my shame and my regret. I'm so sorry I denied you. Surely, as you peer into my heart, you know that I love you!"

As unpleasant as the line of questioning was, Jesus had to go deep. Peter was a mess, and Jesus needed Peter to see that. Jesus is not the kind of doctor who takes a glance at his patient and offers a prescription. No! He diagnoses the problem before offering the remedy. There was no way for Peter to move forward until he came to terms with his failure. Peter sinned when he denied Jesus, and unaddressed sin is isolating in its effect on our lives.

Turning Back

It's common for us to want to move forward after we've messed up. We naturally want to avoid the issue rather than deal with it. We'd rather go fishing on our own than experience the discomfort of what awaits us on the shore. God doesn't rub salt in our wounds or kick us while we're down, but he does reveal the wound and the fact that we're not okay.

> Our personal pains are pathways for the gospel. In our pain we see our need for Jesus.

When our mess is the culprit, we need to identify it, own it, and repent. Our personal pains are pathways for the gospel. In our pain we see our need for Jesus.

The word "repentance" means a change of mind and heart. It is a turning from sin and a turning to God. The word isn't used in this passage, but it's a necessary element of being restored to fellowship with God. Repentance is hard at first, but it produces precious life-giving fruit in the end. Turning away from God seems easier at first, but it produces destruction and ultimately death. Sin seems easier because of its accessibility and acceptability. It's accessible because it dwells within our human nature and the world in which we live. To make matters worse, it's also socially acceptable. Sin of various sorts, such as pride, greed, and lust, are not only accepted but oftentimes praised and encouraged, making sin a potent and persistent adversary.

The power of sin can be illustrated by an episode of *Our Planet*, a nature documentary on Netflix. In episode 1, the documentarists follow a large group of flamingos and their chicks on an African salt pan. One particular chick gets the attention of the narrator. As this tiny flamingo walked, salt began to build up around its ankles. With each step the chick slowed down dramatically and the salt buildup increased all the more. It came to a point where the baby could no longer keep up with the group. The salt became like cement blocks around its ankles and the baby falls behind and can hardly step. The camera pans away and moves on as we're left to presume what happened to the baby flamingo. Without anyone to rescue it, the chick surely died. The scene is gut-wrenching because the salt buildup began with very little but ended up paralyzing the tiny flamingo.

The same is true of sin. Sin starts out small but quickly slows down our spiritual steps and makes us veer off the path. Then shame smothers us. It tells us that God is through with us. It says we're beyond repair. It says that we're a failure, and it sucks hope from our souls. However, turning back toward God brings freedom from shame. It reminds us that our acceptance before God is not determined by our successes but upon Jesus's faithfulness. And through faith in him, we can be restored to fellowship with God. He began a good work in us, and he doesn't intend to quit (Philippians 1:6). Repentance prevents sin from festering in secret and gives the wound an opportunity to receive true healing from the Great Physician.

Get Back to Work

In the midst of Peter's shame and guilt, Jesus offers him life. Each time Jesus asks, "Do you love me?" and Peter responds, Jesus follows up with a command: "Feed my sheep." He doesn't leave Peter in a shame-filled existence; rather, Jesus restores Peter to his calling. He tells Peter, "Get back up. I still plan on building my church and using you to do so. You returned to fishing for fish, but I still want you fishing for people. Your failure hasn't negated your calling because your calling is contingent on my faithfulness, not your successes, so get back to work."

Many followers of Jesus have experienced the kind of failure that brings their lives to a sudden halt. That may be where you're at. You've really blown it. While you know that

God is good and gracious, you wonder if he is good and gracious to you. You feel that your failure is so monumental that it cannot be overcome. One thing we learn from Peter's mess and the subsequent shame he experienced is this: God's not done with you, even when you are done with you.

Through confession and repentance, turning back toward him, you are offered restoration by God to come back to fellowship with him. With faith in Christ, the gifts and calling of God cannot be revoked (Romans 11:29). You belong to God, and no one, including you, can pluck you from his hand (John 10:29–30). Your failure hurts and the pathway to restoration may be arduous, but in God's economy, spiritual growth follows our faith-filled response to pain.

When our youngest son Levi was six years old, he started complaining that his legs hurt. He would go to bed sore from his hips to his feet. Our daughter Keziah and other son Lukas used to make similar complaints when they were his age. These pains worried us when our older kids were younger, but by the time Levi came around, we had learned that these discomforts are part of their physical growth. They were growing pains. Little kids want to enjoy being taller, stronger, faster, and be able to do things that older kids can do like ride a bike, swim, play sports, act, and dance. But these things can't be enjoyed the same when they're four or five years old as when they're nine, ten, or eleven. Growth through pain is necessary, but worth it. So, when Levi moaned, we could calmly and confidently say, "I know it hurts, but good will come of it."

Spiritual growing pains exist for people of all ages. Sometimes it's the product of personal sin and other times it's the consequence of living in a broken world. The pain we experience in life will cause us to grow in our faith if through it we hold on to Jesus. Pain precedes progress and aching precedes change. Through it, God will refine your faith and define your calling.

> Pain precedes progress and aching precedes change. Through it, God will refine your faith and define your calling.

God's not done with you, even when you are done with you!

I love how Jesus ends his conversation with Peter. While he tells Peter that moving forward won't be easy and that difficult times are on the horizon, he also tells him, "Follow me" (John 21:19). Peter was to continue fishing for souls, continue feeding the flock, and continue following Jesus. Although it hurt, Jesus restored Simon Peter, the son of John, also known as the Rock, back to him.

God wants to use you, no matter what you've gone through. He wants to rescue you from the salt buildup of shame and guilt. When you taste grace and are freed from regret, you can freely sing Kelly Clarkson's breakup lyrics: "Since you been gone, I can breathe for the first time. I'm so movin' on, yeah yeah!"[30]

Day of Pentecost

We know Jesus's Sea of Galilee encounter with Peter (John 21) was transformational as the book of Acts picks up the story of the disciples. In the book of Acts we see unveiled what Jesus intended by Peter's nickname. Peter would be the Rock upon which Jesus would build his church.

Just ten days after Jesus went into heaven (Acts 1:6–11) came the day of Pentecost, also known as the Festival of Weeks or Feast of Harvest, a religious observance for the Jewish people marking the completion of the grain harvest. In droves, Jewish pilgrims scattered throughout the Roman Empire, returning to the Holy Land in celebration of this holiday. Peter and the rest of disciples were all gathered in Jerusalem waiting for the gift from God that Jesus promised (Acts 1:5).

We read about a day of Pentecost unlike any before or since. On that day, the disciples were together in one place celebrating the holiday. God the Father poured out the Holy Spirit who descended on every disciple of Jesus (Acts 2:1–4). This was God's plan that Jesus spoke of in John 15:26 when he said, "But when the Helper comes, whom I will send to you from the Father, the Spirit of truth, who proceeds from the Father, he will bear witness about me." The disciples had heard Jesus say it was to their advantage that he depart from them in order to send the Spirit (John 16:7). The Holy Spirit's arrival marked the beginning of a new way of operating. Everyone who turns from their sin and puts their trust in Jesus will be saved and receive the Holy Spirit. The Spirit gives believers a new life through Jesus, guarantees their eternal life, and radically empowers believers to testify about the good news of Jesus. The Son, Jesus, ascended into heaven (Acts 1) after going from death to life and then the Spirit descended from heaven (Acts 2) in order to move people from death to life.

When the Spirit of God came at Pentecost, he created quite the scene. About 120 followers of Jesus were gathered together for prayer when a mighty wind rushed through the room and what appeared to be flaming tongues of fire "rested on each one of them" (Acts 2:3). Although we don't know exactly what they said at that moment, we do know everyone there began declaring God's mighty works. The large crowds that filled the Jerusalem streets for Pentecost saw the commotion and heard their words. The travelers didn't know what to do with this unique scenario. Some were attracted to the things being said while others mocked them, supposing them to be drunk.

The first words we hear spoken from a Spirit-empowered disciple are those of Peter. His words are lucid and bold. His words are unintimidated by the moment and unfazed by the hostile crowd. Peter's quickness to speak up may not come as a surprise. He is often the first of the disciples to say something. But what should surprise us is the manner with which he spoke. Consider this, just fifty days earlier Peter vehemently denied Jesus three times and kept a safe distance from him. Now, he's poised to confront Jesus's detractors and offer forgiveness to thousands.

Follow Me

What changed Peter? An encounter with the risen Jesus, receiving forgiveness for his denials, being told again to follow Jesus, and receiving power from the Holy Spirit—these made all the difference. The Holy Spirit is the stamp of God's saving activity and the power at work in and through us, his followers. Peter believed the resurrected Jesus could resurrect an unbelieving crowd. He told them how Jesus was the Savior of the world who had conquered death. He appealed to them, saying, "Repent and be baptized every one of you in the name of Jesus Christ for the forgiveness of your sins, and you will receive the gift of the Holy Spirit" (Acts 2:38). Peter's boldness is as remarkable as the response to his words. Three thousand people believed in Jesus that day. And so, on the day of Pentecost, Jesus's breathtaking declaration came to pass: "Upon this rock, I will build my church."

Our lives are surrounded by temptation and spiritual warfare. The battle for our faith is real and we can't let our guards down. Because when we do, we make ourselves susceptible to sin and failure along with the painful consequences of guilt and shame. Life becomes a mess. Even still, when we are faithless, God remains faithful because that is his nature (2 Timothy 2:13). He didn't give up on Peter, and he doesn't give up on any of his children. His patience endures in ways we can't comprehend. But this much we know, the resurrected Jesus has the power to uproot our regret and unleash our purpose as disciples. He is the victor—worthy of all praise!

Humor me for a moment as I put Jesus' greatness into comic book language, so you can Marvel at this. Let me tell you about the one who went far from home, so that when it seemed there'd be no way home for us, he made a way. Let me tell you about the true Iron Man whom death could not defeat. Sin has created a Civil War in our soul separating us from God. But God is the Guardian of the Galaxy, the Avenger of his righteous plan. Jesus is the Great Physician, the doctor of the sick, the doctor for the guilty, the doctor for the lost, the doctor of the strange and estranged. Jesus is the Author and Perfector of our faith, the Captain of our lives, the Captain of America, the Captain of our continent, the Captain of all creation. We can't keep this low key (Loki). At the cross Satan thought he had won the Infinity War but little did he know, it was his End Game! Because Jesus lives, our shame and regret can be replaced with real forgiveness and renewed hope.

SAUL, SAUL, WHY ARE YOU
PERSECUTING ME?

7

At the End: Jesus Completes the Story

And falling to the ground, he heard a voice saying to him, "Saul, Saul, why are you persecuting me?"

—Acts 9:4–5

I remember as a kid putting two strong magnets together and watching them stick with force. I enjoyed flipping them around and observing how they would no longer connect. No matter how hard I'd squeeze them together, they wouldn't join. It felt like there was an invisible marble between the two. The magnets would swivel from side to side and not bond. Magnets have a magnetic field around them enabling them to stick to other metals. The north pole of the magnet always sticks to the south pole of another magnet. But when the north pole is placed up against another north pole, it repels. It pushes the other magnet away with force, refusing to connect.

This simple illustration serves as an example of spiritual resistance to God. Our hearts function a lot like magnets. We are repelled from God and attracted instead to things of this world that resist the way of Jesus.

Maybe as you're reading this you can think right away of ways you have resisted God. But perhaps you're on the opposite end of that spectrum and you would hardly see yourself as someone who repels God like two north pole magnets. Resistance to God can be subtle, like ignoring the Holy Spirit's voice to flee a compromising situation and remaining in it. Resistance can be as overt as rejecting God and actively working to oppose his people. Whether subtle or overt, it is, in either case, resistance.

Imagine a resistance scale where on the right side you have blatant disregard for God and open ridicule of people who claim to follow Jesus. On the left side of the scale, you have less obvious resistance, like ignoring God or choosing to believe in Jesus on your own terms. Between those two poles are countless examples of resistance, such as justifying your gossip rather than repenting of it, not speaking up about your faith when God called you to, omitting certain biblical commands because they make you uncomfortable, openly hating the church, compartmentalizing your secular life from your faith life, and twisting the Bible to make it say what you want it to say rather than what it actually says.

Passive resistance to God is often characterized by ignoring him or not following Scripture. Active resistance is characterized by openly pushing God away. All of us resist God at different times in our lives. That's why we all need to learn from the story of this one man who fiercely resisted Jesus but nonetheless found himself drawn to Christ at the most unexpected time and in the most unexpected place.

A Ruthless Adversary

Saul, one of the most ruthless adversaries in the early years of the Christian faith, hated Jesus. He hated Christians. And he hated the possibility that Christian ideas might spread in Israel and its surrounding regions. He proactively explored ways to make life difficult for Christians in an attempt to silence the good news.

Raised in a pious Jewish family, Saul was instructed by the best teachers in Judaism, among whom was Rabbi Gamaliel, a Pharisee. The Pharisees were a revered religious group in the Jewish community. The name "pharisee" comes from a Greek word meaning "the separate ones," referring to their separation from all things ceremonially and morally impure. They were strict in their keeping of the law, including a stringent application of what was not allowed on the Sabbath. The Pharisees created laws to protect laws that heavily burdened people who tried to keep them.

It's like the parent who tells their child they can play outside so long as they don't run in the street. But then, because of the fear of the street, the parent changes their mind and says the child must stay within five feet of the front door. Still, realizing that the front door is "outside" the parent changes their mind again and tells the child, "Actually, just stay in the house." But the house is still in view of the front door, so the parent says, "Come to think of it, I prefer you stay in your room." Finally, while in the room, the parent considers, "While in the room, they may open their door and step out to the living room where they will see the front door of the house and possibly step outside beyond five feet away and end up in the street." So, the parent concludes that the kid should stay in bed to make sure they're safe. This is a restriction placed upon a restriction to protect the original "law" of not going into the street.

Of course, this is a bit of an exaggeration, but it's not too far from Pharisaic Judaism. It was strict. It was rigorous. And it was zealous. Gamaliel took Saul under his wing and tutored him in Jewish laws and Scriptures through a Pharisaic lens (Acts 22:3).

Gamaliel had influence, which gave Saul early prominence for a man his age. However, Saul departed from his rabbi in one important way. Gamaliel chose not to pursue silencing Christianity. He took the position that if it was not from God, God himself would put an end to it. But if it was from God, the last thing he wanted to be found doing was opposing God (Acts 5:34–40). Saul did not have the same kind of patient temperament. He was zealous for the law and vehemently opposed any movement that threatened how he saw things.[31]

The Climax of Resistance

The message of the resurrection of Jesus spread like wildfire in the months after Pentecost. The apostles and other followers of Jesus, under the empowering influence of the Holy Spirit, skillfully demonstrated that Jesus's life, death, and resurrection were all part of God's plan. These Christians also lived compelling lives. The Holy Spirit produced fruit in them in such a way that attracted people from all backgrounds, not just Jews. Saul hated this, which explains why he despised a disciple named Stephen.

Stephen is described as a devout Christian who was full of the Holy Spirit, which meant that his words and actions were gracious and powerful. He performed miracles that authenticated the gospel message he preached. People were attracted to Stephen's God and the message of saving faith in the resurrected Jesus. But not everyone agreed. Some sided with the Jewish religious leaders and debated against Stephen, trying to undercut and disprove his beliefs.

These challengers grew frustrated with their inability to outreason and disprove Stephen. They became offended by Stephen's message that told them they needed to repent of their sins. Consumed by their jealousy and hatred, they condemned Stephen to death by stoning. These haters took off their garments like a man takes off his jacket before throwing a ball at carnival game. The Bible tells us that they laid these robes "at the feet of a young man named Saul ... and Saul approved of his execution" (Acts 7:58, 8:1). Saul not only watched after their garments during the stoning, he fully endorsed it.

A Painful Irony that Hits Close to Home

The sermon Stephen gives before he is condemned to death crescendos when he calls his opposition stiff-necked. He tells them that they have uncircumcised hearts and ears. He adds that they always resist the Holy Spirit, and then he chastises them for being the ones who received the law of Moses but were ultimately blind to its teaching. He says that they are the people "who received the law as delivered by angels and did not keep it" (Acts 7:53). Just as their forefathers rejected the prophets, so they rejected Jesus. They should have known better.

Notice what Stephen is saying. These people had God's word right in front of them. They knew the Scriptures and openly chose to reject their doctrine by their way of life. They heard the truth but didn't walk in it.

The painful irony in this rebuke is that Stephen describes a cultural religiosity that parallels the cultural Christianity found in the West today. This cultural religion in itself is a form of resistance to God. It is playing the part that gets you accepted in the believing community without genuinely caring about the things that God cares about.

Cultural Christianity allows people to form their own tribe with people who believe like them, look like them, worship like them, and act like them. They walk in a collective blindness that inhibits them from discerning their own failures so that they can truly follow Jesus and obey his teaching.

Saul was surrounded by people who knew God's word but refused to hold each other accountable to following it. They loved to uphold laws but neglected mercy. Jesus talks about those who neglect the things closest to God's heart. Consider this rebuke of the scribes and Pharisees—religious leaders like Saul and those who stoned Stephen. Jesus says, "Woe to you, scribes and Pharisees, hypocrites! For you tithe mint and dill and cumin, and have neglected the weightier matters of the law: justice and mercy and faithfulness. These you ought to have done, without neglecting the others. You blind guides, straining out a gnat and swallowing a camel!" (Matthew 23:23–24).

Ouch! Jesus points out that they nitpicked one thing and overlooked the greater things. When we pick and choose what aspects of God's commands we obey and strain out the parts that make us uncomfortable, we become like an editor with a red pen, slashing out parts we don't think fit in. However, we do not have the freedom nor authority to do that with God's commands. We do not know better than God.

This is resistance to God. God has a will and has clearly communicated it to us through his holy Scriptures. When we rationalize why we don't obey it or reinterpret it to mean something more palatable to us, we become "stiff-necked" and "uncircumcised" in our hearts and ears.

The most worrisome aspect of the Pharisees' and scribes' resistance is that they were doing so *within* the community of the people of God. To apply it in our own day, these are people in the church, leaders of the church. They are gathering for worship on Sundays. They are quoting Scriptures. Like the religious voices that rejected Stephen, they decide that orthodoxy (right doctrine) is more important than orthopraxy (right living).

Even as I write this, I'm cut to the heart. I can't help but see how I, too, am in the line of sight of this rebuke. Like most people, I long for ease and naturally resist things that make me uncomfortable. However, the truth is uncomfortable at times. God's commands, while not burdensome, are nonetheless imperatives that call for action that can make us uneasy.

God tells us to love our enemies. He tells us to do justice and love mercy. He tells us to plead the cause of the fatherless. He tells us to be patient with others. He tells us to be quick to forgive and slow to anger. He wants us to extend grace to people who hurt us. He calls us not to rejoice in other people's pain but to weep with those who weep. Let us remain alert and vigilant, keeping close watch over our hearts because resistance can look as fierce as Saul's hate or as subtle as the crowd's complicity. Both register on the scale of resistance to God.

A Chain Reaction

Stephen's murder triggered a widespread persecution of Christians throughout Jerusalem. Saul gladly participated. He spearheaded efforts that went house to house arresting Christians. He dragged them out of their homes and threw them in prison. He was not partial in his actions. Both men and women met his menacing hate.

Saul "was ravaging the church" (Acts 8:3). The word "ravage" is a colorful depiction of the injury done to Jesus's followers. This word is used in antiquity of wartime land decimation or to cause bodily or mental harm to an individual.[32] Saul's ambition was to eradicate the stain of Christianity from Judaism. He would let nothing get in his way.

Saul was on the extreme end of the spectrum of resistance to Jesus. He went out of his way to suppress the Christian message. Murder and threats were like oxygen to him. He inhaled hate and exhaled violence. It was a badge of honor for him to be known as the man who locked up Christians. So deep was his animosity that he was even willing to inconvenience himself to imprison Christians. Saul sought written permission from the high priest to arrest Christians 150 miles away from Jerusalem in the town of Damascus where many Christians fled after Stephen's martyrdom (Acts 9:1–2).

Saul had permission to extract Christians from their homes and return them, bound, to Jerusalem. While his plan was to remove them from Damascus, his true goal was to evict faith from the residencies of their hearts. He wanted to strike fear into all of Jesus's followers, causing them to turn from their faith and thus extinguishing their witness.

The Right Way

The name given to the early church was "the Way." It likely came as a result of Jesus's declaration that he is the only way to the Father and the Christian conviction that they walked in and proclaimed the way of salvation (John 14:6). By rejecting the Way, Saul went on his own way. He chose his own path of resistance to Jesus. However, as he traveled to Damascus, his life would change for all of eternity.

Accompanied by an entourage of soldiers on horseback, Saul was approaching Damascus when a sudden bright light shot through the clouds, knocking him off his "high horse" and bringing him to the ground in sobering humility. A voice from the heavens followed: "Saul, Saul, why are you persecuting me?" (Acts 9:4). Confused, Saul asks for the voice to identify himself. "I am Jesus, whom you are persecuting. But rise and enter the city, and you will be told what you are to do."

The resurrected Jesus met Saul on his avenue of resistance with a question. Like the scores of questions from Jesus we have in Scripture, this one turned Saul's eyes inward.

There are several elements in Jesus's question. First, he asks Saul *why*. Saul is left to consider, what is it about Jesus and Christians that causes him so much hate? Furthermore, Jesus wants Saul to think about why he is *persecuting*. Why has he approved of an execution and aggressively imprisoned people? His hate has led him to physically harm others. But the last element of Jesus's question is the most provoking. He asks, "Why are you persecuting *me*?"

By this point, the resurrected Jesus had already ascended into heaven. Saul wasn't persecuting Jesus per se. However, by causing harm to the people of the church, Jesus counts that as causing harm to him. Jesus's question makes a statement. The Bible tells us that the church is the "body of Christ" and Jesus is the "head" (Ephesians 5:23). When someone resists the church, they are resisting Jesus himself. Likewise, when a person rejects the body, they are rejecting the head also. By persecuting the church, Saul was persecuting Jesus.

Probably more startling to Saul than the question Jesus asked him was the fact that Jesus asked a question at all. Dead people don't ask questions. The one Saul confidently thought to be dead was alive. Saul tried to silence Christians and their claim that Jesus had risen from the dead, but all along, Jesus was doing the silencing. He silenced the arrogant boast of death and silenced his critics. The grave had no voice and no victory over him. Now, Saul, like being in the middle of the ocean, had no ground to stand on.

Jesus likened Saul's resistance to kicking against goads (Acts 26:14). A goad is a long, sharp instrument that looks like a spear. They are used by plowmen who walk behind oxen to keep them in line. When an ox drifts, the plowman jabs the ox to bring it back in place. The more stubborn the ox, the more painful the thrust. What an image! Essentially,

Jesus told Saul that the more he resisted the more poking he'd get. Each blow would increase in pain with every stubborn move.[33] The poking is not cruel, but merciful, as it would save his life.

How could Saul resist any longer? How could he deny what his own eyes had seen and his own ears had heard? In the blink of an eye, Saul's heart shifted, and he was persuaded of the reality of the resurrection of Jesus.

Don't Leave God Out of the Equation

I'm allergic to mathematics. It doesn't like me and I don't like it. I often joke that I became a pastor so I didn't have to deal with math in college. The only "numbers" I work with is the one in the Bible before Deuteronomy. What makes math so difficult for me is that you can work out nearly every step in a complex equation correctly but err in one place and get the whole problem wrong. If you skip a step or do a part incorrectly, you can't get the problem right.

Saul made an error when he left God out of the calculation. He tried to solve the problem, not realizing Jesus was central to the solution. But as the Master Teacher, Jesus helped Saul to see the correct way to solve his problems. It was as if he'd said, *Saul, you made a mistake in your calculation. This equation doesn't include me. But I'm the only one who can help you. I can divide your heart and subtract your pride. I can add genuine surrender. I can multiply your faith. Your life right now doesn't represent a fraction of what I want to do with you. But with me as the solution, belief equals salvation for your soul.*

Whether you find yourself keeping God at arm's length or someone you care about is, don't leave God out of the equation. On this road of resistance, the one Saul hated became the one Saul loved. A miraculous reversal unfolded and the unthinkable was realized. Saul didn't pursue Jesus. Jesus pursued Saul. With Jesus anything is possible.

> Saul didn't pursue Jesus. Jesus pursued Saul. With Jesus anything is possible.

Jesus infuses Saul's life with new meaning. A change of direction takes place in Saul's life, signified by the word "but." Jesus says, "But rise and enter the city, and you will be told what to do." Saul had accelerated toward Damascus with a plan in mind, but he was met by an opposing force who redirected his course and propelled him in the opposite direction.

The magnitude of God's grace is irresistible. His patience and kindness exceed our opposition. When we see his mercy in full view, we can't help but reassess our lives, confess our need for him to change us, express our gratitude, and invest our lives in his service. Your response might sound like this, *God, I was in such a mess. I pushed you away and wanted nothing to do with you. But you were persistent in your pursuit of me. Thank you for loving me like you do and offering your forgiveness beyond what I deserve. I'm all yours. Use me to accomplish your purposes and bring yourself much praise and glory through my life.*

Let's Redirect Our Zeal

However, Jesus isn't finished. Saul would later in his life tell us that when our God begins a good work in us, he intends to complete it (Philippians 1:6). While the risen Savior was busy pulling Saul close, he also visited a man in Damascus named Ananias. Jesus gave Ananias the job of telling Saul what was next for him. Ananias trembled at the mention of Saul's name. He knew Saul's intentions to persecute Christians and wanted to avoid him, as did every Christian in Damascus. However, Jesus tells the frightened disciple, "He is a chosen instrument of mine." The resurrected Jesus is at work. He explains to Ananias that Saul's life will never be the same. God was going to take Saul's hateful zeal and put it to work for his good.

Ananias was given the opportunity to relay this message to Saul. He does so by calling Saul "brother," indicating that he was now in the family of God. Ananias told Saul that he was God's hand-picked instrument to spread the message of Jesus to people throughout the Roman Empire. In accomplishing this mission, he would face adversity and struggle but also experience joy and hope. These are the kinds of things God does when he makes us into a new creation. Through Jesus, the old us is gone and the new us has come.

I live eight blocks from the Chicago-based Radio Flyer wagon company which boasts the largest Radio Flyer red wagon in the world.[34] It sits at the front entrance of the building overlooking Grand Avenue. Originally built in 1997, this gigantic wagon is twenty-seven feet long by thirteen feet wide. It weighs a whopping fifteen thousand pounds and is made of six tons of steel. The wheels alone are eight feet tall. It was inspired by an older, larger version constructed for the 1933 World's Fair held in Chicago. Radio Flyer wagons are known for their durability and have as solid a reputation as the record-setting wagon that sits on Grand Avenue.

One day I explored what had catapulted Radio Flyer to this reputation. I learned that from 1942 to 1945, during World War II, many American manufacturers were asked to alter their production from their traditional product to something that would assist the war efforts as the nation was in crisis. For Radio Flyer, they stopped producing wagons and started producing something called a blitz can. The steel that was previously used for one purpose was now used for another. Blitz cans were five-gallon, steel containers mounted on the backs of jeeps, trucks, and tanks, designed to transport fuel and water to troops stationed overseas. At home, Radio Flyer's war efforts sparked newfound confidence in their line of products. Advertisements began to highlight the classic strength, durability, and dependability of the Radio wagons.

Did you catch that? They were known for one use of steel but then got a new purpose for it. They entered into a war and contributed to the victory. Their purpose had shifted and it produced a new reputation. This is what happened to

Saul. Saul had been known as a man of zeal, using his passion as an enemy of the church. But when he encountered Jesus, he got new orders, a new purpose, and a new mission. God took that same resistant and hateful zeal and turned it into a humble and convinced passion. Saul's purpose shifted and so did his reputation. God halted Saul's hateful production, to bring about something new. Saul would step into a spiritual war by contributing to God's work of saving lives.

When Saul seemed too far gone, he was miraculously brought near to God. He was a persecutor who became a preacher. Saul wanted to put Christians in chains, but God gave him a message that would break chains. Saul excelled in hatred, but God would teach him to love his enemies.

What's Holding You Back?

What Jesus did for Saul he can also do for you. Our former ways of life can be redeemed by God and turned around to be used for his glory. When he does that, we are thrust into a spiritual battle. There is truly an enemy called Satan who roams around like a roaring lion seeking to devour Christians (1 Peter 5:8). But we're not alone. Our mighty Savior Jesus Christ walks with us, shapes us, and

> We're not alone. Our mighty Savior Jesus Christ walks with us, shapes us, and unleashes us fully empowered by the Holy Spirit.

unleashes us fully empowered by the Holy Spirit. In Christ,

we are made new. Still, many of us find ourselves reluctant to fully surrender everything in our lives to Jesus—holding on to various forms of resistance.

Let's get personal. What's holding you back? While I don't know the source of your resistance, I do know the enemy of your soul is creative in his deceit. His lies want to infiltrate your thinking, and unless you filter those voices in your life through God's Word, you will become vulnerable to Satan's trickery.

God wants to insert himself into your story, even when you're not looking for him. That was Saul's case. You might find yourself somewhere on the scale of resistance as the result of disappointment with God, unanswered doubts, frustration with the church, or straight up unbelief. God knows how to navigate those struggles and intervene. He saved Saul's life and he can save yours. With God, all things are possible (Matthew 19:26).

Gaby and Joann's Story

My close friend Gaby was born in Puerto Rico. He spent his teen years playing sports and making a name for himself on the American football field. In high school he got hired at a local department store stocking shelves. One day while stepping into the store elevator, another employee mistakenly summoned it while Gaby hadn't fully entered. The elevator door closed with Gaby pinned to it. As it ascended up the shaft, it took Gaby with it. He broke his jaw and arm and

had many other fractures and injured muscles. This hor-
rific accident made the local newspaper and ended Gaby's
athletic career. He was in the hospital for a month recover-
ing until he was well enough to be released in a wheelchair.
Although he was thankful to have his life, he equally felt
like he had lost it. Once he got home, depression set in. He
began to abuse the prescribed pain killers and added mar-
ijuana into the mix. These were his best efforts at quieting
his anxiety which snowballed into other forms of drug abuse.
During this time, he met his wife, Joann.

Joann came from a single-parent home and was raised
by her dad in Chicago. As a youth she battled feelings of
rejection and abandonment and got into a lot of trouble.
As a solution her dad sent her to Puerto Rico to live with
her grandma, only deepening her feelings of rejection. She
felt life wasn't worth living and at sixteen years old tried to
end her life. Like Gaby, depression and purposelessness
ruled her mind. She lived like this for years. By her early
twenties she was a single mom with toxic friendships in her
life. These "friends" led her to drugs. At that time Gaby and
Joann met. They were two wounded people who attempted
to silence their pain with destructive substances.

As a couple, their lives spiraled and their drug use deep-
ened. It was their way of numbing pain and dealing with
the hurts of their past and present. Gaby and Joann were
in this bondage for years. They lost everything. On one
occasion Joann went to their living room to watch TV when

she realized they sold their TV to buy drugs. At this point, they nearly lost their kids, they had no money, no jobs, and seemingly no future. They had nothing.

However, one night Joann cried out to God, saying, "God, I need you to help me." The next day her sister who lived in Chicago called to tell her she was visiting Puerto Rico in twenty-four hours. Upon arrival, her sister saw Joann's tragic circumstances and took action. She got Joann a plane ticket and returned to Chicago with her. A couple months later, Gaby and the kids joined her. With this intervention, life began to look better. They slowly sobered up from their drug addictions, but they didn't realize they had a bigger problem. Even though their lives were clean, their souls were stained. They were still lost in their mess without Jesus.

Once in Chicago, their five-year-old son Guillo began asking a lot of faith questions. "God told me he wants us to go to church," he would tell his parents. They thought he was losing his mind and hearing voices. Guillo said, "I just know it in my heart that God wants us to go to church." At the same time, Gaby and Joann had some Christian friends, Tony and Lymari, who had just planted a church. These friends frequently shared the gospel with them, but Gaby and Joann didn't want to hear it. Lymari would call Joann to tell her about Jesus, but Joann would literally hang up on her. Even though they were resistant, God was persistent.

For three years, Guillo continued asking his parents to take him to church until one day he got his mom to promise that she'd do so. It wasn't spiritual interest that moved her but simply following through on a promise she made to her son. She took him to Tony and Lymari's church. That Sunday she showed up and could sense a kind of sweetness about the people there, but she continued to keep God at arm's length. She had no intention of returning for a second visit, but God was tugging at Joann's heart. There is no place on the scale of resistance that God cannot work!

She eventually took Guillo to that church again. This time, she was on her Damascus Road. The first song they sang was called "Came to My Rescue." Joann heard the lyrics: "I called, you answered, and you came to my rescue." She immediately remembered that night in Puerto Rico years before when she prayed, "God, I need you to help me," and how her sister visited the next day and pulled her out of that house. She realized that it was God who sent her sister to her rescue. The other song they sang at that service was "You Have Won Me," which says, "You have broken every chain with love and mercy." She then recalled the chains of her drug addiction that no longer held her down. It was God who broke those chains. At that moment, she stopped pushing God away, repented of her sins, and committed to following Jesus. He had truly come to her rescue.

Gaby thought his wife was going through a phase. But she kept going to church and growing as a person. He could see her changing and thought, *I want some of that.* However, his pride kept him firmly on the scale of resistance, and he refused to join his wife. Even though he was still pushing God away, God was persistent. Joann invited Tony and Lymari over for dinner one evening, praying that Gaby would have a great connection with them. He did. His hard heart slowly softened to the things of God. He visited a midweek church service not long after that. While there, he met other men from the church who shared the good news with him. Gaby stopped fighting God, repented of his sins, and placed his faith in Jesus.

Gaby and Joann's Damascus Road was long and winding. Their resistance to God pushed him away for years. They tried to get their lives back together on their own strength but ultimately couldn't. God inserted himself into their story and changed them forever. Jesus met them in their resistance and despair, and they are glad he did. Both Gaby and Joann now have a vibrant passion to live for Jesus and love to tell of God's miraculous work in their lives. Without him they had nothing, and with him they have everything they need. As the two of them walk with and worship Jesus, they're quick to point out that God has given them far more with Christ than all they lost without him.

Gaining More

When Saul believed, he regained his sight and was immediately filled with the Holy Spirit. Empowered by the Spirit, Saul devoted the rest of his life to Jesus by traveling throughout the Roman Empire with this message of God's salvation through Jesus. On one journey, he switched his name from the more Jewish Saul to the gentile Paul as part of his commitment to let nothing get in the way of the message he preached. He who was previously known as Saul of Tarsus would now be known as Paul the apostle.

Paul took the good news and shared his story with men and women while on multiple missionary journeys. He went to major cities like Athens, Ephesus, Corinth, and Rome. In each place he met people who were on the scale of resistance. Through his teaching and testimony to what God had done, people became new followers of Jesus and disciples were strengthened.

However, this work did not come without struggle. What started on the Damascus Road continued on Roman roads marked with suffering. For the sake of the gospel, Paul experienced persecution, rejection, stoning, imprisonment, flogging, abandonment, poverty, and shipwreck. But like Gaby and Joann's story, Paul gained far more with Jesus than he lost when coming to him. He writes, "But whatever gain I had, I counted as loss for the sake of Christ. Indeed, I count everything as loss because of the surpassing worth of knowing Christ Jesus my Lord. For his sake I have suffered the loss of all things and count them as rubbish, in order that I may gain Christ" (Philippians 3:7–8).

Wherever you find yourself on the scale of resistance today, the resurrected Jesus wants to meet you there. Although your pride, resentment, anger, or bitterness may feel too great, God is never out of the equation. There is no mess in which he cannot work. In the blink of an eye, God can flip a magnet so that what previously was in opposition to him is now being drawn to him. Because he lives, your hardened resistance can turn into purposeful peace.

AND BEHOLD,
I AM WITH YOU ALWAYS,
TO THE END OF THE AGE.

8

When Crisis Comes: Jesus Speaks

"And behold, I am with you always, to the end of the age."

—*Matthew 28:20*

As the year 2019 came to a close, visionaries across the globe had a strategy for the coming year. Their 2020 (20/20) vision was well developed and ready to be unleashed when the clock struck midnight on December 31. For the first six weeks of the New Year, many of those dreams unfolded according to plan. But lurking in the background was a pandemic. The novel coronavirus brought the world to a precipitous halt. By the fourth week of March, a significant portion of the United States had shut down. That was the case here in Chicago. Our loud and bustling city became eerily quiet. Churches were relegated to online-only services, schools went to e-learning, employees were forced to work from home, mask-wearing became a mandate, and hoarding toilet paper became a thing. People grieved lost loved ones and lost experiences at the hands of the virus. No one had this written down in their 2020 vision.

Then, on May 25, 2020 another national crisis boiled to the surface. That was the day George Floyd was killed by a Minneapolis police officer, unleashing a greater awareness of an old and present national sin—racism. Peaceful and violent protests followed from Los Angeles to Baltimore, from Chicago to Atlanta, from New York to Portland. Looting and rioting spread in major cities as businesses were burned down. People divided based on how they viewed protesting organizations, law enforcement, and the politicization of this sin. People voiced their opinions and convictions on social media as the fires of animosity spread. No one had this written down in their 2020 vision either. No one expected it.

The year was also a presidential election year. Candidates and parties smeared each other in campaigns. Families became divided over political affiliation. Election results were questioned by many who believed the process was compromised while others saw little evidence of this. National divisions continued to deepen. While many expected this tension, no one expected the United States Capitol building to be breached by protestors two months after the election on January 6, 2021. No one had this on their vision board.

Neither the arrival of the COVID-19 pandemic nor the exposure of the racism pandemic and its subsequent protests nor the extent of the political unrest were on anyone's radar. The news cycles and social media posts became overwhelming for many people and produced a suffocating confusion.

"Where is Jesus in the midst of this mess?" many wondered. The answer is he's right here meeting us. Jesus stepped into our world when he took on human flesh and he continues to step into our lives as the resurrected Savior through the Spirit today. In our bewilderment, he continues to ask questions that draw out our points of struggle. He still delivers penetrating inquiries that reveal where he wants to meet us. We hear those questions by the whisper of the Holy Spirit in our hearts when we read the Bible and commune with God in prayer and worship. He also uses the church and godly people to search our hearts with introspective probes.

The Promise of Presence

After Jesus had risen from the dead and walked this earth another forty days, he took his disciples to the Mount of Olives where he gave them a responsibility and a promise. He told them that their responsibility was to go and make disciples, or followers of Jesus, wherever they were. Christ's disciples recognize their sinfulness, their mess, and their dire need for rescue. We believe that God, who loves people so much, came to earth as a man with the purpose of drawing us to him and saving us from the penalty of sin we deserve. And that's what Jesus did. When Jesus was nailed to the cross, our sins and our messes were given over to him and he took them for us. In this, Jesus became our substitute and paid for our sins when he died on the cross. But Jesus did not remain dead. He silenced the grave and put death to death by returning to life on the third day. He defeated sin, death, and the devil for us. Now, through strength from the Holy Spirit, disciples can turn away from sin and believe in all Jesus accomplished. It is our turn to join with the Spirit to share the good news of Jesus with others and make more disciples who follow Jesus.

Jesus also gave his disciples a promise that is still true for us today. He said, "I am with you always, to the end of the age" (Matthew 28:20). This is the promise of presence. This is a guarantee that only he who conquered death could offer. Because Jesus did not remain dead, he will always live. He will always be able to meet us in life's messes. He will always step into our struggles, asking us questions and comforting our weary souls. I could see him at work in our church family during the craziness of 2020.

Why Are You Weeping? Go.

When the pandemic began to spread and our church was unable to gather in homes or our church building, we felt the pinch in our hearts. We are made for community and to be on God's mission. But how could we be on mission when we were unable to gather anywhere?

Then we saw the mess around us. Our church building is located adjacent to the zip-code area that had the second-highest positive COVID-19 cases in the state of Illinois at the time.[35] Many families suffered. They lost loved ones, they lost jobs, and they couldn't access government assistance due to their citizenship status. They were weary. We grieved for people and were unsure what to do. In those times of prayer and searching, it was the resurrected Jesus through the Spirit who spoke to our hearts, just as he spoke to Mary Magdalene. "Why are you weeping?" Surely, there was great reason to mourn. Things around us were bad, but these challenges also opened doors. Just as Jesus told Mary to go and tell her brothers about the resurrection, it was as if he was telling us to do the same: *In your grief, keep doing my will.*

God opened doors for our church to go and partner with other churches and local organizations to care for thousands in our community with boxed lunches, family groceries, care packages, face masks, Thanksgiving turkeys, and Christmas baskets. We had numerous opportunities to tell people about Jesus and pray over anxious souls. While everything around us was a mess, God stepped into that mess and used us to love our neighbors. In that, he also cared for our hearts. The Spirit breathed life into our weary souls as we got to represent him. Because Jesus is alive, we have a gospel message to share with our words and good news to show with our actions.

Keep Listening

What is God whispering in your ear? Although I don't know what you're going through, I do know that Jesus wants to meet you there. Perhaps it's the sorrow of Mary, the disappointment of the men on the road to Emmaus, the doubts of Thomas, the purposelessness of the men at the Sea of Galilee, the regret of Peter, or the resistance of Saul that relates to you most. Or maybe it's something altogether different. Still, Jesus said, "I am with you always." No matter where you are at or what life is like, keep listening to Jesus's questions. Keep listening to his words of comfort. Keep listening. Why? Because the resurrected Jesus is eager to meet you in your mess.

Study and Reflection

Questions

It's important to reflect more deeply on the ways that Jesus meets us in our mess. This study guide is designed to help you do just that. After reading a chapter, turn to this guide and journal your answers or discuss them with others. This would be a great journey on which to invite people through a book or study group. I'm grateful you've chosen to engage with these questions thinking more deeply on what God wants to teach you from these pages.

CHAPTER 1 – THE RESURRECTED
JESUS MEETS US IN OUR MESS

The entire Christian faith hinges on the fact of Jesus's resurrection from the dead. The Bible says that if Jesus is not alive, then our faith is completely in vain. The reason the Christian faith is so compelling is that there are many reasons to believe that Jesus defeated death and rose from the grave. Just as he revealed himself alive to many people who were in various situations, he does the same for us today. Let's reflect on the hope we find in this amazing truth and why it's important for our lives.

1. Which evidence of Jesus's resurrection has been most compelling for your faith?

2. Jesus used rhetorical questions to cause people to think more deeply about their circumstances and faith as it relates to their relationship with God. What specific question do you think Jesus is asking you as it relates to your relationship with God?

3. Because Jesus is alive, he can meet us in our present struggles. What "messes" in life are you going through right now? Pray and ask God to meet you in those messes in a personal way as you read this book.

CHAPTER 2 – WHEN WE ARE
WEEPING: JESUS COMFORTS US

Mary Magdalene's life was consumed by grief as she came to the tomb the Sunday after Jesus was crucified. Jesus had changed her, and now he was dead. But her life would be forever altered at the sound of Jesus's voice and at the sight of his face. He was alive! Let's consider how we can receive the same kind of comfort in our grief as Mary did in hers.

1. Mary Magdalene lived with profound gratitude over how Jesus had transformed her life. How have you seen God transform you, through Jesus, to be the person you are today?

2. Think of someone in your life who feels like they are beyond God's redemption. How can Mary Magdalene's story breathe fresh hope into them?

3. If you find yourself with your back to Jesus, what is one way you can turn your eyes to him again today?

CHAPTER 3 – IN OUR HOPELESSNESS:
JESUS LIGHTS OUR HEART

Jesus's followers believed he would usher in victory over their Roman oppressors. The things he did and the words he spoke fueled their hopes. However, those hopes were crushed when they saw Jesus executed upon a cross. After his resurrection, Jesus strikes a conversation with two men on the road to Emmaus leaving Jerusalem. As they spoke with Jesus, whom they perceived to be a stranger, they learned the truth that we need, that Jesus knows how to make sense of our confusion. Let's explore how he does that for us.

1. What situation comes to your mind when you think of a time you were painfully confused or disappointed by God's sovereignty?

2. Looking back on those situations, in what ways do you think God was working through them?

3. How have you seen Jesus walk with you (through the Bible, prayer, worship, biblical church community, or the Holy Spirit)? How so?

CHAPTER 4 – DURING TIMES OF
DOUBT: JESUS SHOWS THE WAY

Doubt is an inescapable challenge that confronts people at some point in life. That's what happened to Thomas when the other disciples told him that they had seen Jesus risen from the dead. When Jesus revealed himself to Thomas, Thomas learned that he needed more faith, just like we all do. Let's take a look at how God builds up our faith in the midst of these struggles of doubt.

1. What are the ways you typically respond to doubt when it rises in your mind? In what ways can you relate to Thomas?

2. Which intellectual or practical questions do you feel challenge your faith the most?

3. Even though we can't see and touch Jesus physically as Thomas did, our faith is not blind. In what ways has Jesus revealed himself to you through the Bible and circumstances in life?

CHAPTER 5 – DURING TIMES OF
POWERLESSNESS: JESUS CARRIES US

After Jesus had been crucified and rose from the dead, the disciples did not know how to respond to everything they had experienced. There was regret, disappointment, grief, and then exhilarating hope. When they were back fishing on a boat in the Sea of Galilee, Jesus taught them an important lesson. They needed his power if they were going to live their lives with God's purpose. Let's think through some ways we can apply this same lesson into our own lives.

1. What old ways or habits do you find yourself most tempted to return to? Why is that?

2. What kinds of things do you believe God wants to accomplish in and through you as a reflection of Jesus's "apart from me you can do nothing" statement?

3. Can you think of a time you felt comforted by the words and presence of Jesus? What were the circumstances around that?

CHAPTER 6 – WHEN YOU MAKE
MISTAKES: JESUS FORGIVES

Peter is perhaps the most famous disciple because of his bold statements of faith and his extreme points of failure. We relate to him in a lot of different ways, but one of them is the guilt we feel when we've made mistakes and feel like we've let God down. Jesus meets Peter in his shame reminding him of God's love. Let's listen to those same comforting reminders as we reflect on these questions.

1. Have you ever been sick and tired of your shortcomings? If so, how did you respond to those feelings?

2. Can you identify one or two ways where sin may be trying to build up around your spiritual ankles and slow you down in your faith? How does the gospel of Jesus break that bondage?

3. What has God revealed to you about yourself in the growing pains of life? What have you learned about God during those times?

CHAPTER 7 – AT THE END:
JESUS COMPLETES THE STORY

Saul was an angry opponent of the church. He despised both Jesus and his followers until God grabbed his attention and turned him into a believer of Jesus's resurrection. Saul's resistance to the Christian faith and Jesus's message was turned upside down. We can find ourselves resistant to Jesus in both big and small ways. Just like Saul, we need God to give us a softer heart that's ready to follow his will. Let's consider how God wants to do that for us.

1. Where on the scale of resistance do you find yourself today?

2. In what areas of your life are you most tempted to resist God?

3. Like Saul's passionate hate was changed into passionate love, what things that were part of the "old you" has God repurposed for his glory?

CHAPTER 8 – WHEN CRISIS COMES: JESUS SPEAKS

Jesus continues to meet people in their mess. One way he does that is by using his followers to be his voice by what they say and to represent his hands and feet by what they do. Ultimately, God wants to change our lives and then use us as he changes the lives of other people. Let's discern how he wants to use us to make this kind of impact in the lives of people around us and the community where we live.

1. Which resurrection encounter could you relate to most? Was it Mary in her sorrow, the men in their disappointment on the road to Emmaus, Thomas in his doubt, the seven disciples in their drifting, Peter in his regret, or Saul in his resistance? Explain why.

2. Who is someone in your life that would benefit from hearing the message of this book? What specific resurrection appearance do you believe would encourage them most? Why?

3. What messes exist around you? In your community? How might God be calling you to step into those messes and share the hope of Jesus to people who are there?

Acknowledgments

Writing this book has been a lot of fun and the result of many long nights and early mornings studying the biblical text, wrestling through systematic and biblical theology, and praying through practical implications. Still, it wasn't written in isolation. It's the fruit of the voices and support of numerous people in my life. Thank you to my Brook church family for your regular encouragement and to our elders, Bruce Olson, JJ Pacheco, and Jeremy Barahona, for blessing me with opportunities to write. To my Brook church family, you heard a sermonic version of this book via the pulpit in the spring of 2019. Your affirmations and responses gave me the idea of doing something more with the messages. Thank you. I'm indebted to Todd Hains of Lexham Press for believing in this project before a word was typed out. Similarly, thank you Deborah Keiser of Lexham Press for guiding me along the publishing process.

My dear friend Jeremy Barahona was a sounding board in the preaching and writing process and a much-needed voice. I appreciate you. To my friends Ana Marrero, Gaby and Joann Oyola along with Tony and Lymari Navaro, thank you for allowing me to share pieces of your stories. Your very lives are convincing evidence of the grace and power of the resurrected Jesus.

I write this acknowledgment sitting in my abuela Guadalupe Feliciano's living room. The older I get, the more aware I become of the treasure of my family background and my Puerto Rican heritage. For that, I am grateful beyond measure. In particular, I praise God for my parents, Roberto and Mary Rivera—my papi and mami—for raising me in the faith and always pointing me to Jesus. I am keenly aware that I represent their legacy. In that same vein, I thank God for my sister Ivellise Miller and my brother Roberto "Tito" Rivera. Tito read large portions of this manuscript and offered me suggestions from his own creative writing skillset. He also delivered timely affirmations that motivated me more than he'll ever know.

And to my precious children, I must acknowledge how much you've helped me in writing this book. Keziah, you always show so much interest in this book and ask me many insightful questions which have produced fun discussions about writing and publishing. I hope this work continues to inspire you as the creative writer and future author you are. Lukas, you are a huge encourager who is eager to cheer me on. You never hesitated to ask how things were going with this book. Levi, I love seeing your imagination develop along with your own writing aspirations. Your ideas and stories put a smile on my face and motivated me to press on in these writing goals.

To Erikah, my best friend, the delight of my eyes, and wife. I could not have done this without your support. You've empowered me, cheered me on, read large portions of this book, offered valuable suggestions, and prayed for me. Your gospel fluency insights are interwoven throughout these pages. Thank you for always believing in me.

Lastly, to my good and merciful God—Father, Son, and Spirit—may all who read these pages cast their eyes on Jesus, our mighty Savior who defeated the grave to meet us in our messes.

Endnotes

1. Darrell L. Bock, *Luke*, IVP New Testament Commentary Series (Downers Grove, IL: InterVarsity Press, 1994), Luke 24:1–12.

2. Steffany Gretzinger, "No One Ever Cared for Me Like Jesus" on *Forever Amen*, 2020.

3. Steven J. Lawson, https://twitter.com/DrStevenJLawson/status/771131995988426752.

4. "The thought, then, might be paraphrased this way: 'Stop touching me (or, Stop holding on to me), *for* (*gar*) I have not yet ascended [NIV's "returned" is too weak] to my Father—*i.e.* I am not yet in the ascended state (taking the perfect *anabebēka* with Porter), so you do not have to hang on to me as if I were about to disappear permanently. This is a time for joy and sharing the good news, not for clutching me as if I were some jealously guarded private dream-come-true. Stop clinging to me, but (*de*) go and tell my disciples that I am in process of ascending (*anabainō*) to my Father and your Father.' " D. A. Carson, *The Gospel according to John*, The Pillar New Testament Commentary (Leicester, England; Grand Rapids: InterVarsity Press; Eerdmans, 1991), 644.

5. "With the passive voice, the agent (the person or thing represented as performing the action) is no longer the grammatical subject of the clause. The object or recipient of the action takes the agent's place as grammatical subject. The verb appears in the passive voice form, and the agent or means may or may not be expressed. The frequent result of use of the passive voice is that attention regarding the action is placed upon the grammatical subject (recipient) rather than the agent." Stanley E. Porter, *Idioms of the Greek New Testament* (Sheffield: JSOT, 1999), 64.

6. Robert H. Stein, *Luke*, vol. 24, The New American Commentary (Nashville: Broadman & Holman Publishers, 1992), 611. I. Howard Marshall, *The Gospel of Luke: A Commentary on the Greek Text*, New International Greek Testament Commentary (Exeter: Paternoster Press, 1978), 895.

7. Joel B. Greene, *The Gospel of Luke*, The New International Commentary on the New Testament (Grand Rapids: Eerdmans, 1997), 849.

8. Jeremy Camp, "Walk by Faith," on *Stay*, BEC Recordings, Capitol Christian Music Group, Inc., 2002.

9. Anselm of Canterbury was an influential eleventh-century archbishop and theologian who defined theology as "faith seeking understanding."

10. Warren W. Wiersbe, *The Bible Exposition Commentary*, vol. 1 (Wheaton, IL: Victor Books, 1996), 393–94.

11. See Paul Copan and Ronald K. Tacelli, eds., *Jesus's Resurrection: Fact or Figment? A Debate between William Lane Craig and Gerd Lüdemann* (Downers Grove, IL: Intervarsity Press, 2000).

12. Emphasis added.

13. Jerry Pierce, "Resurrection: Author Lee Strobel Talks About Why He Became a Christian," *Decision*, March 31, 2015, https://decisionmagazine.com/lee-strobel-talks-about-the-resurrection/.

14. Among the "outside" sources is Roman historian Tacitus. Writing early in the second century AD, he talks about Nero's persecution of Christians who are named after their founder, Christus, who was put to death under Pontius Pilate. Tacitus then talks about how a "pernicious superstition" broke out again from the Christians, which is likely a reference to the belief in the resurrection. This suggests that as early as AD 116, when Tacitus is thought to write, Christians were known for both their belief in Jesus Christ as their founder and that he was crucified and believed to be alive after his death. See *The Annals*, vol. 1 of *The Works of Tacitus*, Oxford translation, rev. (New York: Harper & Brothers Publishers, 1889), 423.

15. Lee Strobel, *The Case for Christ* (Grand Rapids: Zondervan, 1998).

16. Eric Rivera, *Christ Is Yours* (Bellingham: Lexham Press, 2019), 86.

17. Warren W. Wiersbe, *The Bible Exposition Commentary*, vol. 1 (Wheaton, IL: Victor Books, 1996), 396.

18. D. A. Carson, *The Gospel according to John*, The Pillar New Testament Commentary (Leicester, England; Grand Rapids: InterVarsity Press; Eerdmans, 1991), 670.

19. Eric Rivera, *Christ Is Yours: The Assurance of Salvation in the Puritan Theology of William Gouge*, Studies in Historical and Systematic Theology (Bellingham, WA: Lexham Press, 2019), 72–73.

20. Tyndale House Publishers, *Holy Bible: New Living Translation* (Carol Stream, IL: Tyndale House Publishers, 2013), Mark 14:71.

21. Da' T.R.U.T.H., "Lights," on *The Whole Truth*, Universal/Exist Records, 2011.

22. Chicagoans resist calling our tallest building by its true name, the Willis Tower. We much prefer its original name, the Sears Tower. The Bean is technically named Cloud Gate. It's a large bean-shaped sculpture made of a reflective metal that allows you to see the skyline from its reflection.

23. WGN, "Chicago Named 'Rattiest' City in America for 6th Year in a Row," October 19, 2020, https://wgntv.com/news/chicago-news/chicago-named-rattiest-city-in-america-for-6th-year-in-a-row/.

24. Morgan Olsen, "Chicago Named 'Rattiest City' in the U.S. Six Years in a Row," October 19, 2020, https://www.timeout.com/chicago/news/chicago-named-rattiest-city-in-the-u-s-six-years-in-a-row-101920.

25. Craig S. Keener suggests that fish were more easily caught overnight and often sold in the morning. *The IVP Bible Background Commentary: New Testament* (Downers Grove, IL: InterVarsity Press, 1993), Luke 5:4–5.

26. The Aramaic version of Peter is "Cephas," which also means "rock."

27. Tony Evans, @drtonyevans, February 5, 2013, https://twitter.com/drtonyevans/status/298973214929993728.

28. The Cross Movement, "Off the Hook," on *House of Representatives*, Cross Movement Records, 1999.

29. In the original Greek, Jesus uses the word *agapao* for "love" in the first two requests and the word *phileo* the third time. In each response, Peter uses the word *phileo* for "love" in response. Some Bible interpreters have seen an important meaning in this distinction. They say that *agapao* is a stronger more intimate kind of love while *phileo* is a softer kind of brotherly love. While this may appear true in some circumstances, other Bible commentators have shown

that this distinction is overstated. They contend that John is using these two different words for "love" as a stylistic choice in his prose. I lean toward the latter interpretation. For a helpful analysis, see D. A. Carson, *The Gospel according to John,* The Pillar New Testament Commentary (Leicester, England; Grand Rapids: InterVarsity Press; Eerdmans, 1991), 676–78.

30. Kelly Clarkson, "Since U Been Gone," on *Breakaway,* RCA Records, 2004.

31. F. F. Bruce, *Paul: Apostle of the Heart Set Free* (Grand Rapids: Eerdmans, 2000), 50–51.

32. Wilhelm Michaelis, "Λυμαίνομαι," *Theological Dictionary of the New Testament,* ed. Gerhard Kittel and Gerhard Friedrich, trans. Geoffrey W. Bromiley, Volume IX (Grand Rapids: Eerdmans, 1964–1976), 312. William Arndt et al., *A Greek-English Lexicon of the New Testament and Other Early Christian Literature* (Chicago: University of Chicago Press, 2000), 604.

33. John B. Polhill, *Acts,* vol. 26, The New American Commentary (Nashville: Broadman & Holman, 1992), 503.

34. Radio Flyer, "World's Largest Wagon," https://www.radioflyer.com/worlds-largest-wagon.

35. Illinois Department of Public Health, COVID-19 Statistics, https://dph.illinois.gov/covid19/data.html.

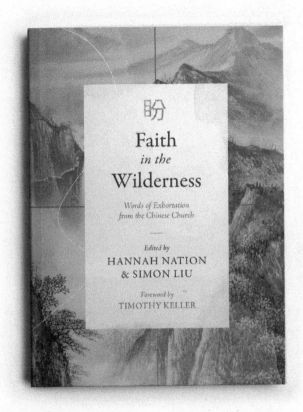